# CHALLENGES PAST, CHALLENGES PRESENT

*An Analysis of American Higher Education Since 1930*

AN ESSAY FOR THE CARNEGIE COUNCIL
ON POLICY STUDIES IN HIGHER EDUCATION

_David D. Henry_

# CHALLENGES PAST, CHALLENGES PRESENT

*An Analysis of American
Higher Education Since 1930*

Jossey-Bass Publishers
San Francisco • Washington • London • 1975

CHALLENGES PAST, CHALLENGES PRESENT
*An Analysis of American Higher Education Since 1930*
David D. Henry

*The Carnegie Council on Policy Studies in Higher Education,*
*2150 Shattuck Avenue, Berkeley, California 94704, has sponsored*
*preparation of this report as part of a continuing effort to*
*obtain and present significant information for public discussion.*
*The views expressed are those of the authors.*

*Copies are available from Jossey-Bass, San Francisco,*
*for the United States, Canada, and Possessions.*
*Copies for the rest of the world are available from*
*Jossey-Bass, London.*

Library of Congress Catalogue Card Number LC 75-24013

International Standard Book Number ISBN 0-87589-265-5

Manufactured in the United States of America

DESIGN BY WILLI BAUM

FIRST EDITION

*Code 7519*

# The Carnegie Council Series

The Federal Role in Postsecondary
Education: Unfinished Business,
1975-1980
*The Carnegie Council on Policy
Studies in Higher Education*

More than Survival: Prospects
for Higher Education in a
Period of Uncertainty
*The Carnegie Foundation for
the Advancement of Teaching*

Making Affirmative Action Work
in Higher Education: An Analysis
of Institutional and Federal
Policies with Recommendations
*The Carnegie Council on Policy
Studies in Higher Education*

Low or No Tuition: The Feasibil-
ity of a National Policy for the
First Two Years of College
*The Carnegie Council on Policy
Studies in Higher Education*

Managing Multicampus Systems:
Effective Administration in an
Unsteady State
*Eugene C. Lee, Frank M. Bowen*

Challenges Past, Challenges
Present: An Analysis of American
Higher Education Since 1930
*David D. Henry*

Presidents Confront Reality:
From Edifice Complex to
University Without Walls
*Lyman A. Glenny, John R. Shea,
Janet H. Ruyle, Kathryn H. Freschi*

# Contents

# Foreword

Ever since Warren Harding gave it publicity in 1920, "normalcy" has been regarded as a condition that is more orderly, more manageable, and more placid than whatever else may prevail at any given moment. And since no one ever seems to see it happen, people assume that normalcy belongs to an older, happier age—the "good old times." This tendency is particularly evident when times are rough.

*Challenges Past, Challenges Present* is an effective antidote for this fallacy. By forcing us to take a hard, realistic look at the condition of higher education during the past 45 years, it makes several trends clear:

1. The past had its own troubles. They might not be identical to those confronted in the present, but they produced similar strains on institutions.

2. Even the best of times have their drawbacks. The author contends, for example, that the "golden years" between 1958 and 1968 were not free of difficulties. They were years of growth, but college and university presidents had as much difficulty convincing the public, legislatures, and donors that growth was occurring and required adequate funding as they now have convincing the same people that the health of their institutions is threatened by inadequate funding as growth expectations diminish.

3. And finally there is "normalcy" of a sort in the continuing struggles of colleges and universities to survive and improve while being threatened by diverse external forces:

changes in the age profile and the socioeconomic characteristics of the population, shifts in career prospects and in the obligations of educated men and women, and changing opportunities for people to take advantage of postsecondary education.

Accepting crisis and change as the rule, and not the exception, may well be the first order of business for those entrusted with guiding the destiny of colleges and universities. The inability to face that reality could be fatal to even the best-intentioned college or university administration.

It is fortunate, for this very reason, that David Henry accepted our invitation to write this analysis of the fortunes of higher education during the past 45 years. He has lived through them as student, teacher, and administrator, culminating his rich experience with 16 years as president of the University of Illinois, one of the outstanding state universities. More than that, he has been a leader of many of higher education's most prestigious national boards, councils, commissions, and associations, and in that capacity has had an important role in shaping the strategies which have helped colleges and universities to weather many of the crises that are the subject of this book. This experience gives wide sweep, great authority, and unusual clarity to the important review he has prepared for us.

CLARK KERR
*Chairman*
*Carnegie Council on Policy*
*Studies in Higher Education*

# Preface

When Cheit wrote of the *New Depression in Higher Education* in 1971, he described the end of a forty-year span of rapid expansion in higher education, from 1930 to 1970. There were several sags in the rising graph line, but expansion was clearly the dominant over-all theme of the period—expansion of enrolments, programs, services, plant, research activities, and scope of mission.

Looking back, one is inclined to forget the many stresses and recall only the momentous achievements. As people grapple with the contemporary uncertainties about higher education, the present way appears rockier, more dangerous, and more difficult. Most of the current publications on higher education overlook the continuing struggle, the repeated crises, the paradoxes, the uncertainties, and the oscillations in .development. Not even the sixties had the affluence attributed to them when added functions, services, and programs are considered as well as enrolments. The record shows that during the years between the "depressions," stability was at times threatened, and the forecasters were as troubled as the analysts of today. (Although technically the economic system has not been in a depression in the seventies, the effects upon higher education from inflation and prolonged recession have been similar to those that occurred in the thirties.)

The purpose of *Challenges Past, Challenges Present* is to highlight some of the changes that have taken place, to note some of the challenges and uncertainties, and to mark some of the responses in the years since the depression of the thirties. In identifying specific changes, methods, and policies, I do not suggest that these be adopted to solve the problems of today. But the experiences of four decades may contribute to an analysis of new necessities. Some myths should be dispelled and some lessons learned. I hope that this book will contribute to those ends. "The past can teach men that they have left Eden or that they are approaching Eden or, indeed, that Eden does not exist and never did. But whatever history teaches, it helps set the stage on which men act. And that has always been its power in human affairs" (Cremin, 1970, p. ix).

Although historically oriented, this commentary is not a history; it is an interpretative essay rather than a comprehensive record. Nonetheless, it is probably subject to the historian's warning that there is a "tendency to oversimplify the past by viewing it strictly in terms of the problems that beset the present (Cremin, 1970, p. xi). In identifying forces and events that have influenced higher education, it has been necessary to make use of generalizations. Such averages do not tell what happened to individual institutions or to each component part above and below a graph line. Both generalizations and data summaries, however, do reflect the climate in which higher education operated, the environment in which each institution charted its own course. Specific references to institutions and segments of higher education will be made, therefore, only when they seem generally representative.

One of the obvious difficulties in writing about higher education is the diversity of the more than three thousand institutions—large and small; public and private; complex and single-purpose; two-year, four-year, and graduate; well-financed and poor; old and new; traditional and experimental—a diversity that is at once a strength and a weakness. There is no system of control or management. The institutions are brought together, nevertheless, by an environment of public expectations, by educational traditions, and by such similarities as sources of financial support and structures of governance.

I thus place emphasis on institutional aspects of higher education such as finance, administration, structure, political relationships, public attitudes. I treat the evolution of educational concepts and philosophies only as reflections of institutional factors. What happened to curriculum development and educational thought as the result of or inducement to change falls outside the scope of this book. It is inevitable, therefore, that the treatment will appear insufficiently analytical for the scholar immersed in a particular aspect of the subject and too condensed for the experienced observer. However, for the reader who was not there, it will be an introduction; for the participant in the events, it will be a reminder.

The focus of attention is on baccalaureate and graduate institutions. The phenomenal development of junior-community colleges is a vital part of higher education in the years under review, but discussing them along with the senior institutions distorts the experiences of the senior institutions. Each influenced the other, but they cannot be viewed as one. (Sometimes this discrimination cannot be made because in many of the data collections, junior-community college figures are included in the summaries for public institutions.) The same point applies to other segments of post-high school education.

In the chapters that follow, I have kept to three main themes: The first is that adjustment to the social environment has been a prevailing characteristic of higher education institutions from the beginning. Sometimes the changes were subtle and slow; sometimes they were highly visible and dramatic. But the impulse to adjust has been omnipresent. Critics in every period have claimed that change happened too slowly, and sometimes the critics were right. Hindsight suggests that rapid action might at times have been beneficial, but it is always easier to proclaim that change is needed than to work out the mechanics of change. Caution often precluded catastrophe, while the institutions grew in number, strength, and importance. The literature of alarm has been conspicuous in every age, but "institutions of society, like species of animals, adapt themselves not in anticipation of change in the environment but in a response to changes that have already occurred" (Ashby, 1974, pp. 145–146). The conclusion is inescapable that the development of higher education may be traced directly to the resilience of institutions in reacting to environmental events, to their capability for response to social demands, and to their constructive interaction with forces that were simultaneously changing society as a whole.

The second theme of the book is that crisis and stress in higher education occur in periods of growth, intellectual ferment, and social excitement, as well as in periods of relative stability or of depression. The colonial period was a time of moderate over-all development, but the crisis of survival for the colleges was real. After the Revolution, the colleges at first shared in the expanding vision and the material opportunities of the new nation. But a crisis of confidence created an uncertain state for higher education from the 1840s through the Civil War, despite the growth of nearly every other social institution. The greatest number of educational achievements from 1636 to 1930 occurred in the four decades following the Civil War, although the ideas for many of these achievements were born earlier. But even though the nation continued to enjoy prosperity after 1900, higher education in the two decades before 1930 has been characterized as "dismal and dreary" (Veysey, 1973, p. 9).

My third theme in this book is that the most troublesome times for higher education institutions have been the years of public lack of confidence in their social significance. The results of such indifference are negative, ranging from enrolment decline to inadequate funding. When such an environment exists externally, it is accompanied by internal confusion and low morale, and the damage is severe. Throughout the entire history of higher education, however, both laymen and educators have appeared as leader-advocates—effective spokesmen to the public. Because of the diversity of institutions and their complex differences, most of these people have been locally influential—institution presidents, trustees, alumni, civic volunteers. Some, however, found national platforms through educational or governmental organizations. In the period here reviewed, strong institutional presidents headed the list: Lotus D. Coffman, Edmund E. Day, Herman B. Wells, J. L. Morrill, and James Killian. Laymen such as Newton D. Baker, Owen D. Young, Devereaux Josephs, and Roy E. Larsen joined the cause. A small number of

leader-advocates were heard above all the others, among them
James B. Conant, Walter Lippman, Paul H. Douglas, and John
Gardner. These and many others have been effective in publicly
identifying the social benefits of advanced learning, the premise
upon which the higher educational structure rests.

## Acknowledgments

I am indebted to Clark Kerr for the opportunity to give my
impressions of higher education during the years of my administrative work with three universities. These institutions were
in the mainstream of stress and crisis during the four decades
described in this book. Kerr's proposal, as chairman of the
Carnegie Council on Policy Studies in Higher Education, was
of interest because the project allowed me to look backward in
a systematic and general way without depending entirely upon
personal recollections of incidents and events. Whether or not
I have fulfilled the expectations for the assignment, the work
has been personally and professionally satisfying.

Earl F. Cheit (associate director), George Hannen (in-
tern), and Verne A. Stadtman (associate director and editor) of
the Carnegie Council were encouraging and helpful in providing suggestions. Eldon L. Johnson, vice-president for governmental relations and public service of the University of Illinois,
whose scholarship, creative criticism, and authorship I have long
admired, read the manuscript and assisted greatly with suggestions for both content and composition.

Bibliographic support has been the work of Stephen K.
Rugg, research associate in higher education at the University of
Illinois at Urbana. In addition, he was helpful in making analy-
ses, gathering data, and providing critical comment. Sharon L.
Hardman was responsible for efficient secretarial preparation of
the manuscript and also assisted with editorial work through
several revisions.

Portions of the manuscript were critically reviewed by
David W. Breneman, staff director of the National Board on
Graduate Education; Jo Ann Fley, associate professor of higher
education at the University of Illinois; Raymond Howes, long-
time officer of the American Council on Education, now re-

tired; Charles V. Kidd, executive secretary of the Association of American Universities; Earl W. Porter, secretary of the University of Illinois; Winton U. Solberg, professor of history at the University of Illinois; and Victor Spathelf, former president of Ferris State College.

Helpful suggestions for the design and approach of the book came from Ernest F. Anderson, associate professor of higher education, University of Illinois; Harry S. Broudy, professor of philosophy of education, emeritus, University of Illinois; Charles G. Dobbins, assistant director, Management Division, Academy for Educational Development, Inc.; William C. Kelly, executive director, Commission on Human Resources, National Research Council; Lyle H. Lanier, director, Office of Administrative Affairs and Educational Statistics, American Council on Education; John D. Millett, vice-president and director, Management Division, Academy for Educational Development, Inc.; Peter P. Muirhead, director, ERIC Clearinghouse on Higher Education; Robert W. Rogers, dean of the College of Liberal Arts and Sciences, University of Illinois; Robert M. Sutton, professor of history, University of Illinois; and Russell I. Thackrey, former executive director, National Association of State Universities and Land-Grant Colleges.

To all the friends and colleagues who have given of their time, wisdom, and insight, I am deeply indebted. Whatever shortcomings may be attributed to the book are due to my failure to take their advice.

*Urbana, Illinois*                             DAVID D. HENRY
*September 1975*

# CHALLENGES PAST, CHALLENGES PRESENT

*An Analysis of American*
*Higher Education Since 1930*

AN ESSAY FOR THE CARNEGIE COUNCIL
ON POLICY STUDIES IN HIGHER EDUCATION

# 1

---

# Trends Before the Crash

---

The effect of the Depression on higher education can best be appreciated when the consequences of those years are compared with previous conditions. The experiences of a student in the twenties would be an appropriate initial focus. His institutional life reflected the development of colleges and universities over a period of nearly three hundred years. We will examine the mood of his time, a mood soon to be drastically altered, and the limitations of the educational structure.

Like all students, the student of the twenties quickly learned academic requirements and expectations, patterns of student life, and the norms of student behavior. But he learned little of the history of his institution or its broad purpose and virtually nothing about the social structure of which it was a part.

More likely than not, the undergraduate had a career motivation, general or specific, that had been stimulated by parents or by high school counselors. Career education was emphasized by numerous professional curricula and, at the university, by professional colleges and graduate departments. The liberal arts student in a general curriculum or in the humanities might have been on the defensive about the wisdom of his choice of program, a choice that often had to be explained to friends and neighbors. Sometimes his choice of liberal arts merely reflected a postponed decision on career. At the same time, the liberal arts student learned that there was a kind of institutional respect for general education and intellectual inquiry into subjects not associated directly with career choice. History could have taught him that in most institutions these were traditional attitudes, not a main contemporary concern.

The student would probably have been the first member of his family to attend college. He was aware that his peers had a growing interest in collegiate life, but he was also aware that college students were a minority and that women were a minority within a minority. The student was not much concerned about the future size of his college or university, although institutional spokesmen expressed pride in growth. At that time, a state university of 3,500 students was considered large.

Since there were few commuting students, most students readily became involved in extracurricular life. Student activities were numerous and varied. Athletics was a dominant interest. Campus attitudes encouraged participation in activities as an important part of education, because of making friends as well as the nature of the experiences. Athletics, journalism, theater, debating, campus politics, hobby clubs, fraternities, honor societies—all were part of collegiate life. Rationale for this pattern was never offered, but the student vaguely understood that the residential campus experience would give him a code of behavior that would mark him as one headed for leadership in professional or public life.

Some programs seemed to go on only because they were traditional. "Chapel" was still compulsory, at least periodically, usually without a religious theme. Courses in mathematics, science, and the humanities were required, but seldom did anyone even try to explain why the hodgepodge of requirements existed. The student appreciated his freedom to choose subjects, open to him more in his upper class years, but no one explained the rationale of the "elective system" or its modified form.

The student of the twenties was not much closer to his faculty than his counterpart 40 years later. Conditions varied among institutions, but the student of the twenties knew that some research professors had few students, that other professors were on a treadmill of repetitive teaching, and that all were living on an inequitable economic scale. Yet there appeared to be relatively little faculty agitation—only a mood of quiet disappointment and reluctant acceptance of an unfair lot.

Dismissals of students were not unusual and were taken for granted as an appropriate part of the scheme of things. Questions of procedural fairness or abuse of authority created no broad concern. There would be occasional demonstrations in which anticollege feeling would be expressed, but such disturbances were generally regarded as horseplay rather than a specific desire for reform. In most places, institutional loyalty was a value from which there was little dissent.

If the student was alert to outside political and social conditions, he knew that literary critics were muckraking the colleges along with other elements of the "establishment" (a word not yet in vogue). Journalists were satirizing the institutions, politicians were suspicious of the social criticism associated with some disciplines, intellectuals were advocating a "new humanism," and parents were fearful about the free thinking attributed to teachers and students. Even though the student did not think about the subject very deeply, he sensed a certain lack of public confidence in aspects of higher education despite public acceptance of educational opportunity as a necessity of "the American way of life."

Although the period was one of great growth, public uneasiness existed that did not reach a crisis of confidence but was expressed in relatively low financial support in the prosperous economy. Within the institutions, the mood was recognized. There was a continuing campus concern for adjustment to the external forces that could bring improvement in support and a greater consensus on purpose and future direction.

This account of a student in the twenties is only a glimpse into the state of higher education at the time. Any brief account would be inadequate in foretelling the tumultuous events to follow or in explaining the long, hard struggle that had brought colleges and universities to this point.

In the colonial era, the pace was slow, the changes undramatic, the attitude toward change moderate. After the Revolution, growth dominated the nation and the colleges shared it to a degree. The tempo of development changed, debate was more vigorous, and a kind of academic nationalism was at work upon the scholastic model derived from the English tradition. But the interaction between the colleges and American social forces did not foretell the future significant role of higher education.

The history of higher education in America before the Civil War was the history of individual institutions. Some survived, others failed. In the nineteenth century, many institutions sought to adjust to the needs of the new nation, but their leaders disagreed vigorously as to the wisest course. Questions arose about curriculum, requirements, admissions, monitoring college life, and identifying purposes.

"Steady state" (or "moderate state") in the colonies and "growth" in the young nation did not seem to make much difference in building support for the institutions. What did make a difference, particularly in the nineteenth century, was resilience to changing social needs, search for identity, and confidence in the future. The missionary zeal of educators to take the cause of the institutions to the people, beyond the social barriers of the times, and to the decision-leaders in all sectors of life made for development (Tewksbury, 1965, pp. 3–9).

Among educational historians, there is a consensus that the 1860s are "a suitable point in time to consider the beginning of the present system. It was then that the first definite steps towards secularization of the American college and the modernization of its curriculum were taken" (Ben-David, 1972, p. xiii).

Educational developments of major significance may be chronicled in the period following the Civil War. Veysey (1973, p. 1) describes them as constituting an "academic Revolution." The curriculum was generally opened to science. The elective course system became popular. More professional and technical programs were offered emphasizing career preparation as a fundamental purpose of higher education. General or liberal education encompassed the classical and the base for the humanities was thus enlarged. Graduate education was organized and research became a part of institutional and faculty purpose, a development greatly influenced by the German university model. Coeducation became a reality. The "collegiate culture" became widely accepted, and it was officially endorsed and encouraged as a part of the informal education of the student. Athletics and student activities in varied abundance became a basic part of college life. While these developments were present in varying degrees in all institutions, large and small, public and private, college and university, the phenomenal growth of the land-grant system was the most dramatic expression of the period after 1860.

Enrolment growth matched the numerous educational changes. The number of institutions increased from fewer than 500 in 1870 to over 1,400 in 1930. Total enrolment grew from between 20,000 and 30,000 to more than 1,100,000 during the same years. Most institutions were far from stable financially, but they could no longer be described as impoverished (Handlin and Handlin, 1970, p. 43).

Enrolment growth was, of course, a response to more than educational change. That suitable programs and facilities should match student and public expectations was essential to public support; an influential social environment was also essential.

Except for occasional low spots in the general economy, the period between the Civil War and World War I was comparatively prosperous. Rapid industrialization was added to an increasingly effective and scientific agriculture. The belief grew that a college education would "pay off" in later life. Social mobility was for everybody appropriately educated. The concept of the personal "usefulness" of an advanced education, referenced vaguely in colonial days, now became personal and specific. "Industrialization altered the structure of opportunities available to young people. The rewards of success were fabulous and the penalties of failure totally disastrous. The widening gap between the two possible outcomes increased the hazards of competition in a dynamic and therefore unstable society" (Handlin and Handlin, 1970, pp. 45–46). Furthermore, the need for credentialing in a complex society came to be widely felt.

The structure of institutions was altered to meet new needs arising from size, complexity, growth, and social importance. Veysey (1973, p. 3) sums up:

> The revolution of the late nineteenth century quite
> simply created the American university (and the

undergraduate college) much as we now know them. The product of a mere trickle from the rapidly rising stream of wealth in the society, the new university nonetheless suddenly acquired a prominent place in the American imagination, and along with this a surprisingly definite (some might say rigid) form. The uniformity of arrangements inside these new or reformed institutions deserves notice, as does the absence of conscious, careful debate . . . about these structural devices. The numbered course; the unit system for credit; the lecture, recitation, and seminar modes of instruction; the departmental organization of learning; the chain of command involving presidents, deans, and department chairmen; and the elective system of course selection all emerged in an astonishingly short period of time and with relatively little variation from one institution to another. . . . The smaller colleges, admittedly, were very uneven in the speed with which they surrendered to the elective system in the years between 1870 and 1910, but it was believed that there was only this one direction in which they could move.

The remarkable growth of institutions after the Civil War and the numerous academic changes were a response both to the increasing complaints about the old colleges and to the current social and economic changes. The developments reflected "a more democratic philosophy which recognized the right to learning and character-training of women, farmers, mechanics, and the great aspiring middle class" (Rudolph, 1962, p. 245).

From the vantage point of the present, there is a tendency to overemphasize the seemingly sudden shift in development. In comparison with the colonial era and the century after 1770, the changes came rapidly; but they were spread over the 40 years between 1870 and 1910—a period as long as between the depressions. There was time for oscillation, for conflict, for dissent, and most important for the development of consensus. A crisis nearly emerged from the opposition of leaders in private education to the growth of the public universities. Eliot of Harvard and McCosh of Princeton were openly critical, and the few devotees of the "classical" colleges did not acquiesce quietly to the new curriculum with scientific, professional, and technical education on the rise.

By 1910, however, the new way was stabilized, although the stability between 1910 and 1930, apart from enrolment growth, was interrupted by World War I. "Throughout the academic year of 1916–17, the colleges and universities were in a condition of uncertainty. The world crisis threatened a crisis academic. This uncertainty and critical condition showed itself in manifold forms. No form was more insistent, or more alarming, than that relating to income and to the number of students attending as a basis of income" (Thwing, 1920, pp. 40, 46). Uncertainty changed to grim apprehension as enrolments dropped approximately 20 percent in 1917–18 from the base of the preceding year.

The response in many instances made use of "the present necessity" to step up efforts to increase resources, and the efforts succeeded remarkably. A time of "public doubt, anxiety, and fear" (Thwing, 1920, p. 54) stimulated activities and plans geared to anticipated postwar conditions. Had the war lasted longer, there might have been long-lasting damage to higher education. As it was, the crisis passed without the institutional structure being harmed seriously.

Changes in education were numerous during wartime—in curriculum, mode of administration, relationship with government, academic freedom, the development of professional education and applied research, and external service. Most of these and other adaptations had their beginning earlier; wartime accelerated their acceptance on the academic scene and in public expectation.

The record is clear that World War I created a crisis for higher education. The threat to stability, even to the continuation of institutions, was real. The response was vigorous, imaginative, and united, making for new interaction with government, industry, and other segments of the social scene and for higher public appreciation of the developing "system."

Apart from the war, the two decades before the Depression are seen by some as a time of no progress, when "lesser men" succeeded the "giant leaders" of the earlier period, when new "academic managerialism" compromised to avoid the threatened division within the academic community and to "cope with the sudden onset of uncertainty" (Veysey, 1973, p. 9). Others see the slow-down in change and innovation as a fortunate interlude for adjustment and gradual adaptation (Kolbe, 1919, p. 3; Brubacher and Rudy, 1968, p. 465).

There were problems enough: insufficient funding in a prewar and postwar growth period that left the faculty and supporting staff under a continuing financial threat. The dimension of growth is revealed in the U.S. Office of Education enrolment statistics compiled for the *Biennial Survey of Education* and reported by the American Association of University Professors (1937, p. 221): The overall gain in enrolment from 1889–90 to 1929–30 was from 156,756 to 1,100,737, or 602 percent. The decagonal percentage increase was 52 percent in 1899–1900, 50 percent in 1909–10, 68 percent in 1919–20, and 85 percent in 1929–30. Obviously, the 10-year figures mask the fluctuations in enrolment caused by World War I; nevertheless they present demonstrable evidence of enrolment growth early in the twentieth century.

There were troubles in addition to finance. With the rise of the muckrakers, journalistic and philosophical attacks were common. And the public resented the student rebellion of the twenties which expressed itself in antireligion proclamations, in defiance of authority, and in a behavior code that jarred. "The lost generation—self-proclaimed—flaunted its interest in sex and whiskey in defiance of the Puritans and of the prohibition laws and provided a compelling model for college youth" (Handlin and Handlin, 1970, p. 69). It could have been that a "crisis of confidence" was in the making when pushed aside by the Depression, just as the crisis of the 1850s was interrupted by the Civil War.

In considering higher education after 1910, one should take note of the birth and growth of national interinstitutional organizations between 1900 and 1920. Two were established earlier, but were thereafter actively important. The list is impressive (Bowyer, 1962):

| | |
|---|---|
| American Association of Land-Grant Colleges and Universities | 1887 |
| National Association of State Universities | 1895 |
| Association of American Universities | 1900 |
| College Entrance Examination Board | 1900 |
| American Association of Collegiate Registrars and Admissions Officers | 1910 |
| American Alumni Council | 1913 |
| Association of Urban Universities | 1914 |
| American Association of University Professors | 1915 |
| American Educational Research Association | 1915 |
| Association of American Colleges | 1915 |
| National University Extension Association | 1915 |
| American Association of Collegiate Schools of Business | 1916 |
| National Association of Women Deans and Counselors | 1916 |
| State Universities Association | 1917 |
| American Association of Colleges for Teacher Education | 1918 |
| American Council on Education | 1918 |
| American Council of Learned Societies | 1919 |
| National Association of Student Personnel Administrators | 1919 |
| American Association of Junior Colleges | 1920 |

The establishment of so many important organizations in such a short period is another index to the times. As institutions grew in complexity, their leaders felt the need for clearer definitions of changing goals as well as group identity. They found stimulation and help in sharing experiences through meetings and in interchanges with critics and observers. Institutional administrators also felt the need for a platform to a larger public and to representatives of government and civic leadership. Finally, several organizations that survive today were born in the wartime sense of common purpose in serving the nation and from the need for joint intelligence and unified action. The general move toward national organizations preceded the entry of America into the war, however.

The American Council on Education is a prime example of the conditions that led to the formation of a national educational association. The initial stimulus for its establishment came from a resolution of the Association of American Colleges calling on President Woodrow Wilson "to take steps looking toward the immediate comprehensive mobilization of the educational forces of the Nation for war purposes under centralized administration, which would coordinate effort and stimulate defensive activities." After preliminary planning by a few leaders, representatives of fourteen national associations organized in Washington, March 26–27, 1918. The representatives adopted a name, elected officers, arranged for quarters and staff, and planned the first annual meeting for December of that year (Dobbins, 1968, pp. 2–4).

The usefulness of the council in wartime quickly led to activities related to other problems and concerns. The goals were defined by Samuel Capen, the first director, in 1921: "The development of the American educational scheme has been planless, haphazard. We have always suffered because of this planlessness. The price that we are called upon to pay for our lack of forethought and consequent lack of system becomes heavier year by year. Unified action has always been impossible because there was no unifying agency. There has been no means even to create a consensus of opinion. A unifying agency has now at last been established. To stimulate discussion, to focus opinion, and in the end to bring about joint action on major matters of educational policy—these are the things that the American Council on Education was created to do. . . . This is the justification for the Council's existence, or there is none" (Dobbins, 1968, pp. 7–8).

In the search for coordination, the group of institutions was taking on the characteristics of a "system." A system in the European sense never developed; nor does a system exist now in ways the public or Congress or legislatures think is operative.

There is no centralized management, planning or control, no single authority. Diversity is a cherished value and considered a protection of essential freedom. Nevertheless, overall progress is dependent upon a degree of consensus. In recognition of that need, voluntary alignment through organizational activities and mechanisms came to play an important role in the development of higher education, particularly after 1930.

# 2

---

# Effects of the Depression
# and Recovery

---

From the preceding overview of American higher education from 1636 to 1930, one may infer that the crises and stresses that threatened the stability and evolutionary development of higher education, even the existence of some institutions, were of two kinds: first, those that endangered the life of the nation; second, those that arose from public skepticism about the values of higher education, from a lack of confidence reflected by indifference or hostile criticism.

The first type of crises includes only the wars—the Revolution, the Civil War, and World War I. With the survival of the nation at stake, higher education was engulfed in the miseries, dislocation, and apprehension that applied to all segments of life. In each instance, however, the postwar era was marked by physical growth of the system, and often educational development was rooted in the social changes and ideas that preceded the war.

The peacetime periods of stress—when doubt and criticism appeared to be in the ascendency—included the 1760s, to be diffused by the Revolution; the 1840s and 1850s, to be obliterated by the Civil War; and the late 1920s, when the national crisis of the Depression became overwhelming, although critics of education stepped up their attack.

The Depression of the 1930s was the first peacetime occasion when the life of the nation appeared to be as threatened as in wartime and when survival seemed even less sure. The effects on higher education would be profound and lasting.

It is a truism that individuals have short memories for unhappy events. Even when tragedy or crisis is recollected, the dimensions of its meaning are modified by time. When identical or similar conditions reappear, old reactions recur without awareness of the similarities to other days or years. However, when one examines the record of the nature and consequences of the Depression of the thirties, he has no difficulty in finding those similarities.

Although current economic factors differ from those of the Great Depression, the impact on higher education from inflation, rising prices, and increasing unemployment has been accompanied by many of the same conditions—reduction in rate of growth (actual decline in the thirties), reduction in rate of funding with retrenchment in expenditures (as compared with needs and commitments), and a prevailing uncertainty about the future.

The two periods are similar in the failure to anticipate the shocking suddenness of change and in the lack of organization or plan to deal with curtailments. In each period there were those who predicted the approaching storm. These people tried to sound the alarm through studies, case histories, and hastily drawn surveys, but the crisis occurred nonetheless. For 40 years, *depression* has been a dread word, a chapter in history not to be repeated in our time. This may be true for the economy in general, as some economic specialists contend. But the effects of the current economic downturn on higher education have already persisted for a longer period than was true in the Great Depression, and the uncertainty as to remedy remains.

### Enrolments and Budgets

It is almost impossible to make an accurate generalization about the effects of the Depression on higher education because hardships were not evenly distributed. Private institutions suffered reduction in income from endowments, private benefactions, and in fee income from students. Policies of tenure, security, and stable organization were sustained to a greater degree in the private sector, but at high cost. Public institutions suffered from reduced appropriations as well as lower fee income.

The summary data on enrolments, expenditures for educational expense, and faculty salaries from 1930 to 1935 records what happened in general. The data are reported by the Office of Education, in its *Biennial Survey of Education*. The use of such aggregate information, however, masks not only regional differences throughout the country but the most severe hardships suffered by individual institutions.

Following a period of growth in which resident college enrolment tripled between 1910 and 1930 and nearly doubled between 1919–20 and 1929–30, enrolments rose again in 1931–32, although at a slower rate. In 1933–34, however, enrolments declined by more than 8 percent, and enrolments for the summer session fell by more than 25 percent. At only one other time since 1900 had the Office of Education enrolment figures shown a decrease, and that was for the academic year 1917–18, during World War I. The decline during the Depression was equally short-lived, however, and enrolments in 1935–36 surpassed the 1931–32 peak.

Expenditures for educational and general purposes followed a similar pattern. Although specific expenditure figures were not recorded in the *Surveys* until the 1928–30 biennium, a record of changes in income was kept. From it the inference can be drawn that expenditures for educational and general purposes increased steadily throughout the first three decades of the twentieth century.

As with enrolments, expenditures for educational and general purposes did not immediately reflect the full impact of the Depression. Funds spent for these purposes in 1931–32 were, in fact, increased by 10 percent from the 1929–30 level. They then fell by 12 percent two years later (in 1933–34), held virtually stable at that level for 1934–35 (Badger, 1934) and recovered nearly to the 1931–32 peak figure by 1935–36. Table 1 depicts both the enrolment and expenditure data as reported in the *Biennial Survey*.

**Table 1. Enrolment and educational expense trends in institutions of higher education through the depression decade**

| | 1929–30 | 1931–32 | 1933–34 | 1935–36 | 1937–38 |
|---|---|---|---|---|---|
| Enrolment (biennial percentage change) | 1,100,737 | 1,154,117 (+4.9) | 1,055,360 (−8.6) | 1,208,227 (+14.5) | 1,350,905 (+11.8) |
| Educational & general expenditures (biennial percentage change) | $377,903,377 | $418,623,399 (+10) | $366,896,087 (−12) | $416,849,067 (+13) | $475,191,638 (+13) |

*Sources:* Enrolments—U.S. Office of Education (1944, Chapter 4, p. 10), Expenditures—U.S. Office of Education (1941, Chapter 4, p. 31).

Although the capital budget and other "noneducational" expenses were the first to be reduced, cuts in operating expenditures, including faculty salaries, were inevitable at all but the most financially secure institutions. A report sponsored by the American Association of University Professors which examined 125 institutions noted that 105 (84 percent) cut faculty salaries at least once between 1930–31 and 1935–36. Nearly all of the public (95 percent) and denominational (93 percent) institutions recorded salary cuts, while a smaller proportion (65 percent) of the other private institutions did so (American Association of University Professors, 1937, p. 36).

Data on faculty salaries during this period are difficult to obtain. Among the most complete studies available are those conducted by the Office of Education on land-grant colleges and universities.[1] Median salaries for faculty at the 51 institutions in the study followed the pattern of decline exhibited by enrolment and educational expenditure figures. From a peak in 1930–31, salaries for all ranks taken together dropped more than 14 per cent in 1934–35.

While salaries began to recover the following year, they did so at a much slower rate than did enrolments or educational expenses. Even as late as 1941–42, after a decade of change, salary levels for all ranks remained below the 1930–31 peak figures. Table 2 provides the salary histories under review.

### Similarities with Situation Today

Whenever negative conditions are initially approached, there seem always to be a considerable number who pursue an "enclave strategy" (Dresch, 1974, p. 56). They would "shore up" existing practices as much as possible, cutting back as required but hoping to outlast the crisis. The strategy is usually ac-

---

[1] Although these institutions may not be precisely representative of all colleges and universities, the salary data they provide do offer an accurate indication of the trends. Salaries at the strongest private universities of the period were undoubtedly higher. On the other hand, salaries at many small private colleges were well below those shown in Table 2. See the U.S. Office of Education (1938, Table 28, P. 50).

Table 2. Median faculty salaries[a] in 51 land-grant institutions

| Academic yr. ending | 1931 | 1935[b] | 1936 | 1938 | 1940 | 1942 |
|---|---|---|---|---|---|---|
| Professor | $4,513 | $3,775 | $3,951 | $4,163 | $4,245 | $4,302 |
| (percentage change) | | (−16.4) | (+4.7) | (+5.4) | (+2.0) | (+1.3) |
| Associate Professor | 3,362 | 2,903 | 2,973 | 3,189 | 3,272 | 3,324 |
| (percentage change) | | (−13.7) | (+2.4) | (+7.3) | (+2.6) | (+1.6) |
| Assistant Professor | 2,837 | 2,449 | 2,486 | 2,592 | 2,605 | 2,645 |
| (percentage change) | | (−13.7) | (+1.6) | (+4.3) | ( +.5) | (+1.5) |
| Instructor | 2,066 | 1,769 | 1,792 | 1,892 | 1,937 | 1,862 |
| (percentage change) | | (−14.4) | (+1.3) | (+5.6) | (+2.4) | (−3.9) |

[a] All salaries are at nine-month rates. [b] Data not available for 1932/33–34.
*Source:* President's Commission on Higher Education (1947, p. 39).

companied by little future planning or imaginative understanding of change in the making. A recent survey of a number of institutions by the National Board on Graduate Education revealed the presence of a good deal of enclave thinking about 1974 problems (Freeman and Breneman, 1974).

A similar numbed reaction prevailed in the first two years of the Depression of the thirties. Conant testifies: "That we were living in the midst of a financial crisis was, of course, a premise everyone accepted. Yet, no member of the [Harvard] Corporation or of the Board of Overseers asked me about raising money. This is an incredible fact. . . . The problem in those days of catastrophe was how to hang on to what little we had and spend it wisely" (1970, p. 94).

In 1937, a study committee of the American Association of University Professors (AAUP) questioned whether in such a time a two-year lag in adjustment was inescapable; the committee pointed out that many argued that contraction should have come earlier, thus lessening the severity of the later adjustment.

One of the "lessons" put forward in the report was the warning that periods of contraction would recur, that institutions should plan for them, and indeed that expansion should not exceed what can be supported in a period of depression (AAUP, 1937, pp. 184, 486, 216). Stability should be the watchword. This approach ignores social need and public demand, political dynamics, and human nature. But if the warning at least merited examination, there was no evidence in the 1960s that anyone even remembered a forecast of recurring retrenchment.

The most serious impact of the Depression upon higher education was psychological. Academic people as a group were hurt less than other segments of the population—in financial terms, employment, or physical want—and institutions as a group survived remarkably well. But the notion that "security of employment" was a built-in characteristic of academic life was severely jolted. Although large numbers of college teachers were not released, they were aware that the cutback in positions had fallen heavily upon the nontenure group, young instructors particularly. College teachers were also aware that many academic staff found places in newly created federal and state agencies, including emergency units that had posts requiring college degrees. There was continuing fear that the emergency agencies would be liquidated before employment readjustment would take place, but without this federal and state aid unemployment among tenure people would have been much greater. Beyond such apprehension, enough firings had taken place to arouse further misgivings. The cutbacks in salaries (and cutbacks in opportunities for moonlighting, which had grown significantly in the late twenties), while not creating want, did cause invidious changes in status and widened the gap in interprofessional comparisons. The gap ironically always had been justified on the "security" enjoyed. Further, policy changes toward shorter-term appointments became disturbing, and the cutback in the modest savings of most academic families emphasized the inadequacy of pension arrangements and created a new preoccupation with that subject.

Related to the disquiet of many faculties was the feeling that collectively they did not have sufficient opportunity to be involved in administrative decision-making. Faculties were deprived of first-hand information about many institutional conditions and problems, and they often did not have a systematic way to make known their views on such pending issues as were apparent. Faculty involvement in educational decisions had become common before 1930. But with notable exceptions, this participation in governance did not reach into financial affairs or administrative organization. From the nature of the situation, institutional policies were often inadequate or wrong. The fact that faculties were not consulted as much as they desired magnified the ill-effects of error. Hostilities developed, some hidden, and morale was weakened by what faculty members thought were blunders or unfair manipulations.

Faculty-administration disharmony was not born in the Depression, but the stress of the period undoubtedly deepened the divisions. This was inevitable when administrative decisions were having such highly charged direct effect upon home, family, status, and sense of security. There is no evidence that the unhappiness led to much concerted action at the time. But the atmosphere was not dissipated, even in the recovery years, a fact that may have encouraged the steady growth of AAUP chapters and the appearance of the Federation of Teachers, which had its start in the elementary-secondary schools.

The growth in the number of AAUP chapters occasioned special mention in the report of the general secretary in 1939. At that time seven or more active members at one institution constituted a chapter and were eligible to organize as such. Using this criterion, the secretary reported the following growth in the number of chapters: 1933, 227 chapters; 1934, 253 (+11 percent); 1936, 310 (23 percent); 1938, 342 (10 percent) (*AAUP Bulletin,* 1939, *25,* pp. 13–14).

One may also infer that the faculty experience in the Depression was reflected in the subsequent strengthening of faculty involvement in governance through senates, committees, and councils. Other factors were at work, such as the increased size of institutions, the growth of departments, and the increase in curricular changes; but the lack of faculty confidence in administrative decision-making was not unrelated.

The recent drive for unionization, for faculty membership on governing boards, and for other mechanisms to enlarge faculty influence is reminiscent of faculty concerns in the thirties. The steady trend over the years toward the adoption of such arrangements has been given impetus by the new depression.

The agenda for the retrenchment process today are not greatly different from the approaches in the thirties. First was the suspension of capital outlay. Significant public appropriations and other resources for private colleges and universities had been authorized to enable institutions to meet the rising enrolments. The difference between 1929–30, the high point, and 1933–34 was an almost 86 percent decline (AAUP, 1937, p. 184), and even this was with the help of federal emergency funds through PWA and WPA. Federal funds for general capital purposes were aimed at helping the construction industry and relieving unemployment, but public colleges and universities were eligible for grants on a matching basis—and matching money was scarce!

Other means of reducing expenditures were compiled in 1932 by the controller of the University of Michigan (Christiansen, 1934, pp. 729–735). His list, widely used, contained sixteen items: reduction in cost of maintaining and operating buildings and grounds; elimination of miscellaneous expenses not directly supporting instruction of students; undertaking no new construction except where special funds are provided; increasing faculty load by not making appointments to vacancies; reducing expenditures for travel; reducing clerical help and office expense; rearranging courses to enlarge class size or to offer them in alternate years or semesters; postponing purchase of library books; reducing expenditures for publicity bureaus and for university press publications; eliminating or reducing appropriations for publication; postponing or denying all leaves of absence with pay; omitting renewal of annual appointments; reducing extension and correspondence work; reducing expenditures for research; eliminating or reducing extra pay for summer sessions; substituting demonstration lectures for individual laboratory experiments in large courses.

Another compilation started with factors that had recently

occasioned increased costs, implying that economy might begin with them: duplication of programs of nearby institutions; extension service; radio service; commencements; dramatics; athletics. Also included were the factors more related to serving larger enrolments—size of faculties and administrative staff, business management and care of campus (Hill, Kelly and Savage, 1933, p. 21). The lists circulated in 1970 and 1971 were not dissimilar.

Tuition was a center of dispute in retrenchment programing, then as now. Institutions felt that they could not afford the loss in income that would result from lowering charges. Students believed that they were being treated unfairly, since prices generally were falling, and student financial needs were increasing as employment and other forms of student assistance declined. Private institutions felt the loss in enrolment and in fees resulting from their higher charges. Both private and public institutions lost income as enrolment in 1933–34 showed a drop of 8.6 percent from the high point in 1930–32.

Although recovery started fairly quickly, time of despair was long enough to encourage questionable recruiting practices and to intensify competitiveness among institutions. This common experience in two depressions should raise the question of how to generate or make more effective moderating influences in institutional relations. Consortia have had limited success in reaching into basic areas of operation, such as sharing of personnel or dividing curricular offerings. Regionally connected libraries have made no more than a beginning in distributing responsibilities for specialized collections. The interinstitutional sharing of instructional resources has not kept pace with the growth of technology in communication. Classroom and departmental sovereignty still discourage collaboration among institutions in mission and services. The use of regional and state external planning boards breeds bureaucratic and political interference that denigrates the professional expertise essential to a cooperative approach to common problems. How to develop effectively a confidence in the unity of higher education as a whole as a basis for interinstitutional cooperation remains an unanswered question.

The competition of the thirties went beyond student recruitment and created a climate that came to be recognized nationally. "A spirit of institutional self-acceptance rather than a spirit of academic competition and imitation will contribute most to the long-run stability and achievement of higher education in this country. Many of the Depression period difficulties arose because such a spirit was wanting" (AAUP, 1937, p. 96). The competition for status was not always between public and private institutions—sometimes it was between large and small, rich and poor, expansion and steady state, junior colleges and four-year institutions, or between baccalaureate and graduate programs.

The instances of competition or status seeking involving institutional imitation, then as now, and characteristic of the less critical periods, raise a question that must be faced particularly in a "no-growth" situation. Can what Eric Ashby has called "mimicry in higher education" be managed in any way other than through external controls or is mandatory coordination inevitable, with all its threats of intrusion upon autonomy?

The Depression heightened the demand for external coordination, perceived as a means of eliminating "waste and duplication" and lowering costs. The Depression made people conscious of public expenditures and emphasized the politician's dilemma, ever-present but more visible and more difficult to manage in hard times—how to spend more on public welfare and at the same time hold the line or reduce taxes. The tax situation in the Depression was complicated by the heavy proportion of state expenditures supported by the property tax and by the inadequacy of other revenues in the redistribution of funds. In some states, property taxes were limited by constitutional amendment, forcing action on unpopular new sales, consumer, or income taxes to avoid bankruptcy.

The calls for economy were loud and raucous. Charges of extravagance for alleged "fads and novelties" were common. Educators were blamed for conjuring "incredible sums out of the pockets of the people." Growth in enrolments "with attending publicity, may lead to undue haste in making higher education the first target when retrenchment in public expenditures becomes imperative" (Hill, Kelly, and Savage, 1933, p.

21). It was feared that legislators under pressure would find higher education an easier target for reduced expenditures than roads and governmental jobs. Taxpayers' associations prepared lists of economies for legislative consideration. Governors sent messages to legislatures on the same subject. Business and civic organizations passed resolutions endorsing the need for economy in governmental activity, including expenditures for education (Hill, Kelly, and Savage, 1933, pp. 14, 24, 25). The president of the Brookings Institution feared that "Hysterical demands for economy by a tax-desperate electorate may easily become mere parsimony and result in crippling basically important state services, including education" (Moulton, 1933, p. 40).

A first response to the outcry for economy came from state government. Taking legislative concern over alleged high costs as a cue, officers of state government moved to tighten controls of institutional budgets and expenditures. Political departments, eager to expand their domain, then as now did not support the concept of autonomy for colleges and universities and moved wherever they could to impose pre-expenditure authority. An Indiana law in 1932 gave "an outside budget committee wide powers not only over future curricular expansion of institutions, but also over the determination of quality and service of professors, so far as these items are controlled by salaries formerly apportioned by boards upon the recommendation of presidents and their colleagues." In a number of states directors of finance became the chief financial control officers, regardless of the appropriations form (Hill, Kelly, and Savage, 1933, pp. 9–10).

With the public querulous about the cost required for the previous expansion of higher education, the discussion of regional cooperation and statewide coordination of public institutions was intensified. The contemporary commentary refers to numerous studies and programs recommending coordination for efficiency. However, the discussions were not immediately productive. Within states, few educational structures were altered and regional compacts did not appear until after World War II. Some voluntary interinstitutional arrangements were reported in the mid-30s, 115 arrangements involving 230 institutions (Wilson, 1965, p. 74), but the growth of consortia and other voluntary cooperative arrangements was also a postwar development. Nonetheless, the basic idea emerged in the Depression, and one may conclude that the new depression will enhance its appeal. Many critics have educational, administrative and philosophical reservations as to the wisdom of state coordinating and superboards of control, but such reservations and possible corrective measures are set aside in a period of financial stress.

### Federal Involvement

The most important single theme of this entire period was the increasing support of higher education by the federal government, a continuing major consideration in the light of the present need for even greater assistance.

The federal interest in education was first expressed in the Northwest Ordinance of 1785, which reserved public lands for educational purposes. This use of land grants culminated in the Land-Grant Act of 1862, which made possible the establishment and development of the land-grant colleges and universities. Direct appropriations came with the Second Land-Grant Act in 1890, and other appropriations were made before World War I.

The first significant change in scope, direction, and purpose of federal aid to education occurred in 1933 and came almost without design. The Federal Emergency Relief Administration was created to help the states by providing for "work-relief" activity. In Minnesota late in 1933, relief funds were used for students. The idea quickly spread and was applied generally throughout the country in February 1934. By 1935, responsibility for this program was assigned to the National Youth Administration. The program aimed at keeping students off the labor market and had immediate widespread acceptance, even by those who had been skeptical of federal action in the area of higher education.

The grants were of immense importance to students and to institutions. The funds relieved the low enrolment problem, both in public and private institutions. The tuition issue receded somewhat as a primary concern. Students were helped in meeting their personal financial requirements, and the work projects were useful. A student's work assignment related to his educational interests and added to his employment experience in a meaningful way.

A 1937 sampling survey of over seven thousand college aid students in 338 institutions tabulated the following distribution according to type of work (Lindley and Lindley, 1938, p. 165):

| | |
|---|---|
| Research, surveys, statistics, etc. | 21.4% |
| Community service | 20.5 |
| Ground and building maintenance | 16.3 |
| Departmental service | 9.0 |
| Library service | 8.3 |
| Clerical assistants | 7.4 |
| Laboratory assistants | 4.0 |
| Home economics | 2.8 |
| Construction | 1.9 |
| Recreation and education | 1.5 |
| Reproduction (photography, printing, etc.) | 1.3 |
| Art and dramatics | 1.2 |
| Tutorial services | 1.1 |
| Janitorial services | 0.9 |
| Miscellaneous | 2.4 |

"The research, survey, and statistical projects cover a range as wide as the frontiers of human knowledge. Examples selected at random include: experiments in the development of new ceramic glazes; soil research; the preparation of local and state historical studies; transcription of legal debates in foreign countries; the editing and indexing of old manuscripts; the study of building illumination; research in cellular metabolism; the preparation of topographical atlases and of charts and other devices for instructional use; research into an immense variety of economic and sociological subjects" (Lindley and Lindley, 1938, p. 166).

During the eight years of NYA existence, 2,134,000 youths received assistance, 620,000 in colleges, and 1,514,000 in secondary schools (*Final Report of the National Youth Administration*, 1944, p. 82).

The significance of the federal student aid programs in the Depression turned out to be long range. It set the precedent for the postwar educational benefits for veterans—the largest "scholarship program" in history—and for the student aid programs of the sixties and seventies. Furthermore, it opened a way for federal assistance to reach private institutions. Debate on that issue continued into the fifties, but federal policy was made firm by the Higher Education Act of 1965 and the Education Amendments to that Act in 1972. The debate from here on would not be on whether there should be federal aid to higher education, but on what form, how much, and in what proportion of total cost. The nature of federal responsibility is now accepted as regards educational opportunity, including social justice, equalization of regional benefits, manpower availability for national needs, the advancement of knowledge, and funding. The first widening and deepening of those concepts came with the Depression of the thirties, and it may be anticipated that their further application will be accented by the new depression.

The federal role in research support should have special mention. The experience was not an altogether happy one. The emergency agencies, designed for relief assistance, early recognized that CWA-WPA projects in construction and in community service did not meet the employment needs of academic people. A number of "research-oriented" activities were authorized under the direction of colleges and universities—"traffic surveys, housing surveys, electrical-appliance census, standard-of-living studies, and others." Many of them were useful, but they hardly qualified as meeting research standards. Some institutions had more research assistants under their direction than at any time in their history (AAUP, 1937, p. 383). Some programs were ill conceived and came to be included in the opprobrium of boondoggling, an opprobrium that grew with the years. Although the relief benefits to the individuals were clear, damage to the general reputation of academic research was serious and had consequences difficult to measure.

A more positive evaluation may be given to federal relief activity in adult education. Although these activities were organized almost entirely outside colleges and universities, campus

Table 3. Federal relief activity in adult education

| Classification | Teachers | Enrolees | Classes |
|---|---|---|---|
| General adult ................... | 13,029 | 573,166 | 39,480 |
| Literacy ....................... | 5,600 | 189,375 | 15,403 |
| Workers ....................... | 836 | 46,576 | 2,685 |
| Vocational .................... | 4,814 | 207,348 | 14,210 |
| Parent education .............. | 931 | 56,691 | 3,362 |
| Nursery schools ............... | 4,982 | 46,661 | 1,466 |
| Freshman college .............. | 455 | 7,962 | 67 |
| Correspondence study centers ..... | 310 | 14,909 | 596 |
| Other educational projects ....... | 3,483 | 181,456 | 10,643 |
| Totals .................... | 34,440 | 1,324,144 | 87,912 |

*Source: The New York Times,* December 13, 1936.

facilities were utilized. Academic personnel, both unemployed and institutionally assigned, were called upon in large numbers. The local sponsors—school districts, recreation departments, state departments of education—were energetic and imaginative and readily undertook nontraditional educational activities. Artists, musicians, and others with teaching competence were employed along with teachers from all levels of schooling. Many fields of knowledge were covered, the selection being made in terms of local needs and interests. Recreational projects were included and many of these had educational overtones. Table 3 gives some notion of the size, nature and scope of the program.

### Student Reactions

A strident echo from the thirties with familiar overtones in the seventies relates to student unrest. The Depression was a disillusioning experience for most students. Not only were they thrown into the discomfiture of "making ends meet" and sharing in the general worries of their parents' generation, but they felt that their future was uncertain and their aspirations were destroyed. A student speaker at the Harvard commencement in 1933 seemed to reflect the common attitude and was widely quoted: "We have been forced gradually to unlearn a lesson. We have been forced to forsake reluctantly the teachings of the Golden Age. Our four years of college have coincided with the dismal years of the depression. Many of our members have been forced to abandon their studies. Others have been sorely pressed to meet expenses. Some, who never contemplated it, have earned their way. And now we all stand at the end of a road and look toward what?" (Conant, 1970, p. 119.)

Then as now, many tried to explore "the student mind." These efforts ranged from journalistic feature articles to serious studies by social scientists. The results were inconclusive. There was no consensus about how to deal with the prevailing stereotype; student thinking was as diversified as that of the general public. But uncertainty about the future was obviously more crucial to the young, and the atmosphere of insecurity bred criticism of "the system." It was natural that new student groups would appear expressing interest in social problems.

The range in point of view was wide, from criticism of the system to proposals for action, "some conservative, some liberal, some radical" (AAUP, 1937, p. 15). Most were centered on the external scene rather than on the educational institutions. The groups had enough common ground to be termed a "student movement," but their chief common characteristics were their vitality and a "consciousness of kind" rather than militance.

Naturally, those termed "leftists" attracted the greatest attention. There was the tendency in public discussion, in those days as today, to attribute the views, attitudes, and actions of a relatively small number to students in general.

Some of the organizations antedated the Depression. The Intercollegiate Socialist Society, founded in 1905, became the League for Industrial Democracy after World War I. The National Student League broke away from L.I.D. in 1931. The record of such groups and their publications and programs are an interesting chapter in the history of the times. In this commentary, they are relevant only in their parallelism to the more violent student expression in the late sixties, with its residue in the current depression. The advocacy of strikes, of union with labor, of demonstrations against war, of abolition of the ROTC, of opposition to discrimination against minority groups, to loyalty oaths and to any restriction of free thought and free expression were issues that have a familiar ring (AAUP, 1937, p. 318).

"The American Student Union, formed in 1935, as a coalition of Socialists, Communists, and liberals, was to report twenty thousand members out of a student population of over one million. . . . In April 1934, twenty-five thousand students were reported to have taken the Oxford Pledge against participation in war during the student antiwar week. By April 1935, 185,000 students were counted as participants in such demonstrations" (Lipset, 1971, p. 179).

"Free speech" encompassed another set of issues, centering on student rights to campus-based political activity, institutional control of visiting speakers, censorship of student newspapers, and disciplinary action for student participation in demonstrations (Lipset, 1971, p. 180).

That Communists influenced and sometimes dominated student political activism was readily documented. Public concern over Communist involvement with youth groups was widespread and in some ways created more turmoil for institutions than the positions taken by students on specific issues. In the end, however, political radicalism had little continuing appeal and student attitudes did not at any time support violent institutional rebellion. As the effects of the Depression stretched into slow recovery in the late 30s, yearning for economic security took precedence among student interests.

Student activities with social and political impact precipitated public reactions. The authors of the AAUP Report were moved to say, "The inevitable social result of an emergency—economic or political—is a 'push to the extremes.' Black becomes blacker; white becomes more white. The importance of any 'cause' is magnified. Something akin to a 'crowd psychology' develops. This was true in the years following 1929, and the situation has by no means cleared in 1937" (AAUP, 1937, p. 432).

## Public Attitudes

Colleges and universities, by the nature of their function, are pressure centers. They transmit knowledge and they seek new knowledge. Sometimes the two are in conflict, as applied to commonly accepted values. Further, as public agencies in a functional sense, however governed, all collegiate institutions are subject to the pressures inherent in human wants and interests. The most crucial problems come when ordinary pressures are aligned with mass movements.

Three mass movements affecting higher education developed in the twenties, were carried into the Depression years, and even today have some advocates, although with comparatively little force. One movement produced loyalty oath legislation. In World War I days, "It was unpatriotic to be objective" (AAUP, 1937, p. 437). Nonconformity was impossible without serious risk. The abolition of teaching of the German language in the schools will remain an index to the hysteria of the times. The idea persisted that one could enforce patriotism in loyalty oaths enacted by states, with teachers as particular targets. Loyalty oaths were written into the platforms of many organized groups. Loyalty laws were adopted by a number of states, and some of these laws persisted into the 60s, when court decisions finally overruled them. One loyalty form was the disclaimer, requiring an assertion that the signer had not been a member of an organization that advocated the overthrow of the government by force or violence. Other forms required only affirmation of loyalty to the constitution of the state and of the United States, sometimes applicable only to teachers, sometimes to all state employees. Even after public support for such enactments became doubtful and enforcement lax, legislatures seldom took the initiative for repeal. These laws remained sources of agitation, often hampering positive relationships between the legislatures and the institutions, as in Illinois and California. The courts finally found them "discriminatory" or "constitutionally vague."

Another movement was grounded in racial and religious intolerance, best symbolized by the Ku Klux Klan and expressed in attacks on Jews and Asians as well as Blacks. Finally, a popular movement showed concern for what was taught, with specific resistance to the teaching of evolution, climaxing in the Scopes trial of 1925. In the Depression, these and a number of other groups were moved to voice their discontent, some with old roots, some newly planted.

These issues as well as those having to do with finance, mission, and accountability heightened institutional awareness of the need for understanding the goals and purposes of higher education, the nature of the institutional structure, and the importance of higher education to students and to society generally. While external relationships were handled in a local context, there was emphatic general recognition of the need for initiative on the part of institutions to reach out to make positive contact with their special constituencies (such as parents, alumni, employers, the professions) and the public generally. Pressure for unwise economy, for damaging cutbacks in program, for control of student behavior and faculty thinking, and for political manipulation of policies seemed to reinforce the need for a constructive response—improved public interpretation at the local level as well as on the national platform.

The AAUP Report (1937, p. 462) summarized: "It (Public Relations) is the most important matter of them all."

Unfortunately, the general academic community did not rally to this point of view nor effectively encourage universal involvement at the grass roots level. The responsibility for follow-up was left to the administration and to specialists, when the aid of the whole affected group was needed; this is discussed more fully in Chapter 10. Will response in the new depression be different?

### Partial Recovery

In 1939, the President's Advisory Committee on Education report was able to state, "In most cases the worst injuries of the depression have now been repaired, and there is a general disposition to build anew on a sounder foundation" (p. 7).

As noted in Table 1, enrolments returned to the familiar pattern of biennial growth after only one biennium of decline, with the 1935–36 resident college enrolment 4.6 percent higher than the previous high in 1931–32. Education and general expenditures recovered nearly as rapidly, and the 1935–36 figure was within 1 percent of the 1931–32 peak amount. Expenses for these purposes had fully recovered by 1937–38, with a total more than 13 percent above 1931–32.

The recovery of faculty salaries had a much different picture, according to Table 2. Whereas enrolments had recovered by 1936 and educational expenditures by 1938, salaries paid faculty in land-grant institutions during 1941–42 remained below the 1930–31 levels. Coupled with a rising cost of living, the slow recovery of faculty salaries proved one of the most lasting of the Depression effects. As will be noted in more detail later, faculty salaries did not approximate those of comparable professional groups until the sixties.

The tables do not reflect, of course, the many indirect effects of the Depression that lingered on to create other problems. For example, since salary rates did not uniformly come back to previous levels, personnel inequities were inevitable. Promotion and salary advancement of some of the older faculty were delayed as newcomers were recruited. The number of positions did not grow as rapidly as enrolments, so classes were overloaded. Disruptive practices such as "dry" promotions (that is, advancement in rank without financial increases), tolerated in an emergency, were not always promptly terminated or reversed. For students, educational costs were rising as the proportion of economically marginal persons was increasing. Younger faculty members appeared antagonistic to a system that seemed to exploit them through heavy loads, salaries lower than those in other professions, and undue delay in advancement.

There was new competition for resources. Depression agencies sought to continue their own existence. Public expectations for public subsidy had vastly increased in many ways. How would higher education make its case in comparison with social security, unemployment compensation, and housing, for example? Would the required new taxes discourage voluntary giving? What would be the effect of the liquidation of emergency agencies upon academic personnel who were on leave to join them? There was much uncertainty and apprehension, individually and institutionally.

In sum, economic recovery did not bring ready reassurance for the future or a return to the conditions of pre-Depression days. The world was more complex, higher education was more involved in that complexity, and problems were more numerous than ever before.

## Impulses Unfulfilled

Little has been said about educational change in the thirties because there was little significant that could be specifically attributed to the Depression. The experience of the decade does not lend encouragement to the common assertion that out of retrenchment "reform" may be supported, or to the premise that constructive innovation may result from cutbacks. The cutbacks were taken without basic alteration in structure and where traditional practices were disrupted, they were given priority in restoration.

There was, of course, notable educational ferment. The Progressive Education Association reached the campus with experimentation in admissions. The work-study programs were encouraged by economic conditions. Experimental colleges were founded at Sarah Lawrence, Bennington, Wisconsin, and Minnesota, and there were others. Alexander Meiklejohn and Robert Maynard Hutchins were names in the educational news, as were Harry D. Gideonse, Hamilton Holt, and Irving Babbitt, who with others precipitated lively debate on new ideas in education. But only various plans for general education had widespread adaptation. Here both philosophy and economy in instruction were joined, as well as student interest arising from the fact that more specialized education had its employment limitations in nearly all fields. General education had its most influential although not original expression, however, in the famous Harvard report of 1945. Even then, a generally accepted model for undergraduate liberal education has not evolved and many regard the present content as a "disaster area" (Alan Pifer, quoted in Carnegie Commission on Higher Education, 1973b, p. 216).

A more promising outcome for the course of higher education was the widespread success with adult education. Although colleges and universities were not the chief agents in the initiation or administration of the emergency programs, faculty members were involved in many ways and the professional interest was genuine. Many studies suggested that not only had systematic adult education come to stay, but that it offered colleges and universities great opportunities for leadership in service, research, and professional training. The psychology of adult learning attracted attention, supported by successful experiences. Extension divisions and evening colleges in urban universities had acquired considerable experience and the time appeared to be right for institutions to plow new ground, to reach for new constituencies, and to develop the rationale for new and more programs. The State of Michigan recommended: "The Federal Emergency Relief Administration should be used to the fullest extent as a means of laying the foundation of a successful program for the years to come" (Superintendent of Public Instruction of the State of Michigan, 1934, p. 32). The President's Advisory Committee on Education came to the same conclusion and in 1939 recommended that "Special Federal grants to the States should be provided for educational services to adults" and that "they should also be available for expenditure through the extension services of colleges and universities and through other appropriate educational agencies" (Superintendent of Public Instruction of the State of Michigan, 1934, pp. 136–137).

These expectations for adult education programs were not fulfilled, however, partly because of the interruption caused by World War II. The heavy demands later placed upon the institutions by returning veterans—demands largely for conventional programs—precluded the expansion of collegiate adult education except through regular work. The reality of "a learning society" had to await the priorities of a later decade—and the arrival of a new depression for higher education. Will the present uncertainty as to purpose and method and the lack of resources again cause postponement?

The Civilian Conservation Corps was another success of the emergency educational arrangements. Noncollege unemployed youth benefited, as did conservation programs. Educators noted that the project was inherently educational in function and in the character of organized activities. The work-education combination, already encouraged in the college work-study experience, had quick public approbation. The possibility of a continuing youth organization with a heavy leadership and service contribution from colleges and universities was frequently mentioned as a natural post-Depression development (AAUP, 1937, p. 480). As with adult education, however, the war and postwar events pushed aside the opportunity. With the rise in unemployment of noncollege youth in the current period of the seventies, perhaps this national-service impulse of the thirties will be felt again.

Reaching consensus on solutions to educational problems was as difficult in the 1930s as in the 1970s. One of the reasons, then as now, was lack of data and focus.

The 1937 Report of the AAUP study committee on *Depression and Recovery* referred to "deficiencies in the data or to an utter dearth of them." It complained that "there are relatively few sources to which one may turn . . . for well-organized, continuous, quantitative analysis covering the period from 1929–30 to the present." The result was dependence upon opinions rather than substantiated facts. Further, the statement accented the need for prompt reporting, a need stressed by the National Board on Graduate Education nearly 40 years later (NBGE, 1974, p. 81) and even suggested that the chapters of AAUP might well consider going into the data reporting business. "Some of the depression-recovery problems would not have seemed so pressing or led to such uncertainty had there been at hand adequate statistical materials that would have given greater understanding of the drift that was taking place" (AAUP, 1937, pp. 507, 527).

Undoubtedly, a careful analysis of the conditions criticized in 1937 compared with a survey of contemporary problems in data gathering would reveal many improvements. That the criticisms of inadequacy are so parallel and the consequences so enormous would suggest, however, that this impulse of the thirties ought quickly to be revived. Too much is at stake to continue a practice of policy formulation and program building with insufficient information and inadequate analysis.

While many similarities and parallels between then and

now have been suggested, they cannot possibly convey the desperate mood of the people in the early thirties—what Walter Lippmann called "a paralyzing deadlock in our affairs." Lippmann stated, "This sense of hopeless impotence produced a great panic in which men, acting on the impulse of each for himself and the devil take the hindmost, tried to save what they could from the wreck. . . . There is a limit to the endurance of a democratic people. In February [1933] we had reached that limit" (Quoted by Conant, 1970, pp. 118–119).

It was in this setting that colleges and universities had to carry on and still "keep the faith." They were harassed from all sides—by state bureaucracies that imposed repressive controls, by demands for cutbacks in expenditures, by attacks on their nature and function from the radicals of the right and left, by student dissent and faculty distress, by scapegoat treatment from demogoguery on platform and in press. There is undoubtedly a resemblance between conditions producing the loss of priority status in the current situation and events in the thirties—but the virulence of criticism in the Depression far surpassed what is now encountered.

Nonetheless, we must consider the concern expressed on all sides in the commentary of the times and by those who had educational responsibility—that aggressive social interpretation is a major institutional responsibility that must be reflected in institutional action. It will be remembered that faith and advocacy were given high place in the progress of higher education before 1930, a stress that was heightened during the Depression in the search for public understanding and reasoned response to hysteria and unfair attacks. External advisory committees were established, institutional activities in public interpretation grew in scope and number, and national organizations gave increased emphasis to the premise that social progress is dependent upon public understanding—the keystone of institution building.

Those who worked through the Depression and have thought about it in retrospect would say that the present challenge for accountability can be met by renewed concern with institutional interpretation. Confidence in the system is essential to adequate support and can be restored in no other way. Hence, the similarities and unfulfilled impulses have significance beyond interesting coincidence. They reflect some long unfinished business and contain some warnings against indifference to these emergent ideas. Studies and reports are useful, but they are not enough. Higher education operates in a political and social context. More bridges between the campus and the public must be built and the traffic sped up.

# 3

# World War II and Change

The European war began on September 1, 1939. On September 8, 1939, the President declared that "a limited national emergency exists." On December 7, 1941, the Japanese attacked Pearl Harbor. In the intervening two years, it was increasingly apparent that military and civilian preparations were in order. Yet when war began for the United States, there were no national plans for the use of colleges and universities. Some people even suggested that the institutions might as well be closed "for the duration" (Conant, 1970, p. 341).

While the prewar debate over possible U.S. military intervention went on with vigor, there seemed to be little understanding of what involvement actually would mean. "Singapore had fallen, yet we drove our cars on borrowed time; our Navy was under-equipped, but resisted the deprivation of our mechanical conveniences that speedy and adequate preparation demanded; our Army was undermanned . . . yet Selective Service Boards (established in September 1940) were beseiged by requests for exemptions" (Miller and Brooks, 1944, p. 1).

Quite apart from whether and when there should be intervention, educational leaders did speak out on the need for planning. In June 1940, the American Council on Education and the National Education Association jointly formed the National Committee on Education and Defense and charged it to maintain liaison between the government and the educational community. However, as in 1917, "Neither the government nor the college was prepared to articulate the functions of the colleges in modern war" (Miller and Brooks, 1944, p. 1). Two reasons were offered by Conant: "Not only was no agency prepared to make the kind of plan about which we spoke so readily, but the top officials of the Navy and the War Department had no intention of accommodating their plans to any general scheme. . . . Until we knew the needs we could neither plan our educational programs intelligently nor arrange for the deferment from the draft of students and recent graduates" (1970, pp. 339–340). It is probable, also, that the military planners at that point could not exactly define the needs or anticipate very far into the future. Certainly manpower needs in 1944 were far greater than could have been predicted in 1942.

At the beginning of the school year 1941–42, nearly 10 months after the entry of the United States into the war, higher education was confronting a situation graphically reflected in a New York state emergency conference on long-range planning. This is described by Miller and Brooks (1944, p. 150) :

> The conference convened as scheduled. The date was October 17, 1942. The Japanese were landing reinforcements on Guadalcanal; the Navy had just announced the loss of three more cruisers; the Germans were in the streets of Stalingrad and were advancing on the oil fields of the Caucasus. The House of Representatives that day passed, 345 to 16, a bill lowering the draft age to eighteen; on September 12 the War Department had announced that at the end of the current term reserves who had reached the Selective Service age would be called to active duty; committees of educators working in Washington under Presidents Cowley and Day had not yet been able to cut the Gordian knot to release plans for the effective utilization of higher education in the war effort; and reports made public at the morning session revealed 23 percent fewer men in the colleges of the state than the year before. To hard-pressed administrators the

unsolved problems of higher education in the immediate present left no time for the consideration of "A Long-Range Program for Higher Education in New York State." By majority vote the afternoon session was indefinitely postponed.

World War II followed the pattern of the earlier wars and of the Depression—lack of government planning; delay as the nation debated policies and directions; initial wasteful confusion as plans were finally initiated almost on a trial and error basis; and tardy mobilization. In this setting educational planning was impossible.

In January 1942, over one thousand college presidents and other officials met in Baltimore to take stock of the situation, to pledge "the total strength of our colleges and universities" to President Roosevelt, and to define the needs of the institutions in fulfilling the pledge. Miller and Brooks provide the agenda of concerns for action (1944, pp. 31–32).

A national survey of manpower and the facilities of colleges and universities to meet these needs:

Acceleration of college programs.

A study of the extent and bases of federal aid desirable to make such acceleration possible.

A study of and the development of plans for the solution of shortages in teacher personnel and related educational fields.

The maintenance of standards both in regard to admission and to the granting of credit for military experience.

Development of an exchange of information on plans and policies pertaining to defense.

Necessity of increasing concern for the physical fitness of the student.

A study of the academic calendar for both the secondary school and the college.

Endorsement of the principle of Selective Service for the procurement of manpower for the armed forces.

Occupational deferment of selected premedical, predental, pretheological, and graduate students.

"The Washington jungle grew more tangled and dense as the months of 1942 went by. New vistas of hope seemed to open just as it became clearer and clearer that the demands of the fighting forces for very young men were threatening the enrolments of the colleges. . . . The presidents looked forward with dismay to the academic year 1942–43, when there might be little income from student fees" (Conant, 1970, pp. 340, 343). Enrolments had already started to decline because of enlistments, drop-outs for high-paying war jobs, and selective service call-ups. Others who normally would have enroled waited indecisively. It became clear that college enrolments would be drawn from women, men below age 18, those physically ineligible for the draft, and members of the several reserve corps who were urged to stay in college until called. Also, there were some men in campus-based contract programs with the military services. From the peak year 1939–40, civilian enrolments had dropped 41 percent by 1943–44.

Resident college enrolments totaled nearly one and a half million in 1939–40. They dropped 6 percent in 1941–42, and civilian enrolments plummeted another 37.5 percent by 1943–44—the most sharp decline in the twentieth century. Even when students in on-campus military training programs were added to the totals, the figure for 1943–44 remained more than 22 percent below the 1939–40 peak. The upward trend was regained by 1945–46, when returning veterans helped boost the enrolment total more than 12 percent above the high in 1939–40 (U.S. Office of Education, 1950, p. 18).

Nearly every aspect of college and university administration was "war-related." Student "war counseling" became a major activity. Military information was vast, technical, and subject to frequent changes; recommendations for student deferment had to be made with great care. Specialists had to be appointed. At one point the selective service regulations were issued in six volumes. In terms of policy, the framework for later expansion of student personnel advising was constructed with emphasis on the needs of the individual, the relationship of training requirements to ability, and the importance of sound manpower allocation.

Many faculty members left the campus for war-related employment or for government service, both military and civilian. Vacancies had to be filled on short notice from a dwindling supply of teachers.

As fee income declined and costs increased, finances in general were threatened, although the burden did not fall equally on all institutions. There were proposals for emergency government aid for administration, but they did not receive serious legislative consideration. Fortunately, with the help of government contracts and the use of the colleges in military reserve programs, the over-all financial decline halted by 1945–46. To replace fee income, colleges and universities were able to rely on federal and state governments, to the extent that expenditures for educational and general purposes expanded during the war years.

For all institutions reporting to the U.S. Office of Education, student fees accounted for 35.7 percent of all income for educational and general purposes in 1939–40. The fraction was reduced slightly in 1941–42, to 32.6 percent, then cut nearly in half by 1943–44, when it fell to 17.9 percent. Funds from the federal government accounted for 5.4 percent of educational and general purpose income in 1939–40, 8.1 percent in 1941–42, and 35.7 percent in 1943–44. In the latter year, federal funds accounted for virtually identical portions of educational and general income in both public and private institutions (U.S. Office of Education, 1946, chapt. 5, p. 24).

To be sure, much of the increase was dissipated by rapid inflation. Worse, accurate budget forecasting was nearly impossible because of uncertainties in the scope of federal contracts for war-related instruction or services. George Zook, president of the American Council on Education (1943, p. 148), characterized the budget-making process as "a continuing nightmare to all who take [it] seriously." Lack of uniform rates of payment, delays in receiving funds for contract work, and strong differences among institutions in the amounts received for administrative implementation all contributed to the chaos. As Zook bluntly put it, those colleges not selected at all for government contract work "are in a bad way" (1943, p. 148).

There were other organizational problems. Some departments were without students. Some students were without faculty. Early admissions became a common practice. Maintaining standards became a concern, as credit was sought for unrelated military and work experience. Some courses were telescoped. Extra credit was urged whenever possible; credit *in absentia* was provided for students who missed class time because of service. Some requirements were lessened. The accelerated calendar was widely adopted and accelerated courses followed. Even liberal arts education made the effort to adjust its curriculum to a wartime context (Miller and Brooks, 1944, p. 54). History and geography were stressed. The fundamental unity of knowledge in the complexity of world problems became a general education theme. Transdepartmental presentations for a "broader outlook" in general or liberal arts education were arranged.

As might be expected, work-study programs, "cooperative education" arrangements, vocational and utility education had unusually heavy student interest. Professional education in fields such as nursing, chemistry, and physics introduced specific wartime-related subject matter. There was a general feeling that "the curriculum will never be the same again" (Miller and Brooks, 1944, p. 102), a judgment that proved correct.

## A Program Evolves

After two years of apprehensive hoping before 1941 and another year and a half of waiting for action, the wartime program had become defined by the fall of 1943. The regular instruction for nonmilitary students was supplemented by organized programs for Army and Navy enlisted and officer personnel.

Contracts for training military personnel were initiated at approximately 660 institutions. The contracts fell into three general classifications: *college instruction* such as the Army

Specialized Training Program, the Navy V-12 Program; utilizing faculty, facilities, and services; *military instruction* such as officer candidate schools, utilizing college facilities and support service but employing military faculty; *vocational instruction* at technical levels such as aviation refresher and training courses. These military contract instructional programs were at their peak in academic year 1943–44, when more than 310,000 students were enroled (Grace, 1948, pp. 210–215). Between 1939–40 and 1943–44, the federal government spent more than $97 million for contract courses related to the military effort (U.S. Office of Education, 1947, chapt. 4, p. 31).

Special contracts providing training for other departments of the government were arranged, including the Civilian Pilot Training Program. The advanced ROTC was expanded. Individual members of the military services reserves were encouraged to remain in school until called to active service. Colleges that did not have government subsidy through such contracts were especially hard hit financially.

The largest and one of the most impressive specially organized programs was the engineering, science, and management war training unit. This program was instituted at the post-high school level to meet the shortage of technical workers, supervisors, and experts in fields essential to national defense (Miller and Brooks, 1944, p. 105). The courses were short and intensive, offered at both the college and subcollege levels. Such courses usually did not carry college credit, but some part-time evening students preferred them to traditional college work. Each institutional proposal reflected the needs of the community and the resources for instruction. The U.S. Office of Education supervised and coordinated the programs. Between 1940 and 1945, nearly 1,800,000 men and women had been enroled (Armsby, 1946, p. 45). The result extended beyond the war period. The popular new adult education pattern had established a precedent for postwar planning (Miller and Brooks, 1944, p. 106).

The colleges and universities reached into their communities in many other ways. The natural desire to participate in the war effort was given form and encouragement by the national project known as Key Centers of Information and Training. The Federal Security Agency recognized that colleges could be centers of influence in their communities in ways beyond their traditional instructional responsibilities. The Key Centers project was set up under the Office of Education.

First efforts went into activities that seemed naturally related to regular duties. First-aid classes, training for air-raid wardens, and centers for blood donations were organized quickly. Public forums, lectures, and conferences with subjects ranging from current affairs to postwar development also came naturally. The general public and students, as well as faculty, were involved in the planning. Libraries, films, radio, exhibits, and concerts were focal points. All community organizations were drawn together into the activity. Individual participation was the key to public interest. Forums, round tables, and conferences reflected a discussional approach much more popular than impersonal lectures by specialists.

A very important outgrowth of the activities sponsored by the Key Centers, both for the community and for the nation, was the inevitable emphasis on postwar planning. By the time the war ended, the public was far better informed about international relations and national concerns for the postwar world than it would have been otherwise—involvement in intellectual activity had been an important morale builder.

The Key Centers were another successful demonstration of the potential for adult education, in this instance largely informal as contrasted with classroom teaching. John Studebaker, wartime Commissioner of Education, was moved to say in 1942, "I have long felt that a real program of adult education is overdue in the United States. . . . The next big area for conquest by American education . . . is this field of adulthood" (*Higher Education and the War*, 1942, p. 58). Studebaker reflected the views of college presidents across the land. These were expressed in a 1944 survey that anticipated a full range of subjects, vocational and cultural, and the use of many channels and arrangements including short courses, radio instruction, and correspondence study (Brandon, 1944, pp. 37–50).

This account of higher education in wartime does not

deal with the research contributions of individual academic scientists, extensive and significant as such contributions were. They were enhanced by the new organizational approach of the National Defense Research Council under Vannevar Bush. Said Conant, who had an important role in NDRC, "I shall never forget my surprise at hearing about this revolutionary scheme. Scientists were to be mobilized for the defense effort in their own laboratories. A man who we of the committee thought could do a job was going to be asked to be the chief investigator; he would assemble a staff in his own laboratory if possible; he would make progress reports to our committee through a small organization of part-time advisers and full-time staff" (Conant, 1970, p. 236). Higher education came to be associated with war-related science activity. The plan was exceedingly effective and pointed the way to postwar use of academic staff and facilities in government-formulated research.

### Transition

One of the most interesting phenomena of the wartime period was the early concern with postwar planning. Before the role of higher education in the war was fully implemented and before victory was assured, leaders were looking to the requirements for adjustment when the war would end. Perhaps the impulse had its root in the need for positive thinking when the fortunes of the allies were at low ebb. The unanticipated call of the ill-prepared campus military for front line duty in 1944 was an indication of the serious manpower shortage. Apprehensions were not often voiced in campus discourse, although they were real. But postwar planning nonetheless was a popular subject even earlier.

The forward look usually began with a concern about how to deal with the returning veterans—their interests, attitudes, educational needs—and the adequacy of the collegiate way of life and of the existing programs to meet those needs satisfactorily. Questions followed about the adequacy and readiness of higher education in general to serve not just the veterans, but the changed postwar population. These considerations touched nearly every conceivable subject from technical and professional education to general education, from community colleges to graduate schools. International relations was also a frequently used planning theme.

In 1943, Isaiah Bowman, President of Johns Hopkins University, said that his only fear was that "the lessons of the war will be lost in the fatigues of a postwar world in which people may try again to find security in provincial simplicities, assumptions, and slogans, educational or otherwise" (Miller and Brooks, 1944, p. 167). The Educational Policies Commission declared in *Education and the Peoples Peace,* "Now is the time for the American people to match the varied wealth of their great resources, and the tremendous military potential of their men and their machines, with a moral and educational program of equal stature" (1943, p. 59).

The commentary in many cases became much more specific. The experience of the armed services in the uses of audiovisual aids to instruction and techniques for the improvement of instruction were examined for campus adaptation. The feasibility of area studies as an appropriate organization of study materials on international relations and cultures was demonstrated. Agenda topics for serious discussion included the values and difficulties of acceleration, correspondence instruction, a new version of general and liberal education, fulfilling the needs for less than degree terminal education, and the expansion of continuing education. Conferences, institutional and statewide planning committees were formulated, as were regional and national forums (McConnell and Willey, 1944, pp. 54–162).

Whether or not acceleration should continue as a permanent feature of higher education was much discussed. The concept of a "speed-up" calendar was a natural development in wartime. It took the form of a 12-month schedule, emphasizing short intensive courses, at times combined with a concentrated week of 20 or more class hours. The idea had been debated before on psychological, physiological, and sociological grounds, but it took the pressures of wartime to bring a plan into reality.

The concentration feature, except in noncredit work for part-time students, was generally deplored by educators but accepted as a wartime necessity (Brandon, 1944, pp. 4–7). Acceleration as a concept, however, found more favor although the education community was divided about the desirability of acceleration as a continuing calendar for collegiate life. Obviously veterans with a sense of lost time should have the option of accelerating their work; but permanent adoption of this form was precluded by the even division of judgment. Opinions varied from "It (acceleration) defeats the ends of normal education" and "Inner maturity is more essential than acceleration" to "Student load should be varied according to student capacity and interest." The "curriculum must be streamlined" was another view, as was "Overlapping . . . should be eliminated by a study of the curriculum as a whole"; but "Students need *time* for a real education" (Brandon, 1944, pp. 4–6).

Acceleration came to the fore again in the sixties, as enrolments exceeded plant capacity. At that time, economy in the use of facilities became the central issue, and it was somewhat persuasive with the public. Some concessions to the proponents of acceleration were made through lengthened summer schools, adoption of the quarter system, the trimester calendar, or similar adaptations. Student and family interest in "speed-up" lagged, however, and faculty opinion was not supportive. As a result, for the majority of students the nine-month school year remained the norm.

The current interest in the three-year degree has revived some of the old discussion. The basic concept of the three-year degree, however, is a revision of content rather than compression of a four-year program. The wartime version of acceleration has persisted only in its availability as a student option. Whether the plan takes on new acceptance will be determined by student and family opinion.

Although many of the problems and developments in postwar higher education had their roots in prewar situations, an Office of Education Bulletin declared in 1945 that "a new leaven" was introduced into college instruction through war training programs. "Whether we like it or not, the war has brought the necessity of a 'One World' outlook on international relations. Schools and colleges face a Herculean task in adjusting programs and minds to produce a generation of citizens and experts prepared to cope with problems incident to living in this altered world comity." On the domestic scene, the war "has augmented and focused the issues in labor-management relations in industry, and has intensified the crucial problems the Nation faces in dealing with race and minority group problems" (Hollis and Flynt, 1945, p. 2).

As early as March 1944, the American Council on Education considered implications of military training experiences for civilian postwar education. The Council wrote to the Secretaries of War and Navy suggesting the establishment of a commission to examine the question. Both Secretaries expressed their support for the plan and promised full cooperation. With financial aid from the Carnegie Corporation and the General Education Board, in 1945 the Council created the Commission on Implications of Armed Services Educational Programs. Under the direction of Dr. Alonzo G. Grace, the Commission published its summary report in 1948. A series of nine monographs treating major subjects considered by the Commission in greater detail also appeared between 1947 and 1948.

The Commission focused on two principal questions: "What can education in America gain from the experience of the vast wartime training effort?" and "What are the lessons for education and the national culture and strength now and in the future?" As an introductory note to its report, the Commission offered some general observations to set the context for more specific discussion (Grace, 1948, pp. 6–7):

1. The Army and Navy training programs may properly be classified in general as *job training and indoctrination,* all colored by specificity. (Emphasis added.) Lessons in methodology for specific training are found, but few lessons for the future in intellectual freedom or a liberal education are noted.

2. Civilian educational agencies, including schools, colleges, and libraries do not have the generous financial support from national sources that the armed services had in time of war. They do not have twenty-four-hour-a-day control over [the student] or

his activities, and the motivating factor of life or death as a result of how well a lesson is learned does not prevail.

3. The armed services necessarily had to operate on a trial and error basis. If a program failed to produce results, immediate changes were ordered. They were not hampered by tradition.

4. Although the Army and Navy developed distinctive methods of training for their purposes . . . the principles applied were generally not entirely new to civilian educators. In the development of wartime training programs, the services of civilian educators in uniform . . . and of eminent educators as civilian consultants were utilized.

Although the Commission gives muted treatment to the subject, it is clear that within the higher education community opinion was divided on whether the military methodology had anything at all to offer higher education. "Liberal arts proponents claimed that education, as distinct from training, is as essential in war as in peace" (Grace, 1948, p. 233). Not surprisingly, those faculty who were concerned with broader and less practical issues, who were interested in a student's capacity for clear thinking and logical analysis, found the mass of military students on campus generally deficient in mathematics, the sciences, and language arts (Grace, 1948, p. 233). Those responsible for training the military students dismissed such criticism as irrelevant, given the original task at hand. The Commission report makes only a brief reference to these differing impressions.

No one urged that the military methodology be adopted generally by college and university instructors. However, the Commission found several implications of the military training experiences which related to college level instruction. The Commission pointed out that war and its aftereffects forced colleges and universities to modify their programs. The changes in American society and worldwide conditions induced by the war made it "impossible to think of higher education and the responsibilities which the atomic age have imposed upon it except in terms of adjustment and redirection" (Grace, 1948, p. 234). The Commission then went on to describe new directions suggested by recent military experiences which higher education might pursue with profit, including these (Grace, 1948, pp. 232–244):

1. *Continue interdisciplinary approach.* The war has made higher education increasingly aware of the need for continuing to integrate knowledge. (The Commission attributed the success of several military courses, including the Army's foreign language and area studies program, to the ". . . nationwide efforts of college instructors, representatives of many disciplines and academic departments, who were able to break the shackles of traditional departmentalization.")

2. *Experiment with acceleration.* The intensive and accelerated nature of the college training programs created the major adjustment that had to be made during the war, and affords an impetus to further practical experimentation in time saving. (The Commission suggested several ways in which the learning process could be expedited, all based upon successful military experiences. They included: (a) credit by examination, especially for the mature student; (b) re-evaluation and reorganization of curriculums, course content, and methods of instruction which could contribute to economy of students' time and efficiency of instruction and learning; (c) creation of special techniques to speed the progress of students whose social or academic backgrounds do not fit conventional molds, but who are above average in intelligence and achievement; (d) fuller utilization of existing plants and facilities by staggering attendance, increasing off-campus instruction, and by special intensive courses wherever appropriate; (e) allowing carefully selected groups of superior students

to proceed at an accelerated rate; (f) expanding and refining individual guidance techniques and opportunities.)

3. *Establish goals and outcomes.* Institutions of higher learning are faced with the postwar responsibility of establishing specific goals and desirable outcomes for their instructional programs.

4. *Improve motivation.* Compensations for academic achievement need to be something more than good grades and paper honors. (The Commission urged that ". . . higher education must make every effort to arrange the course content and the courses of instruction so that they will motivate students to attain their desired and foreseeable aims, cultural and vocational.")

5. *Promote student adjustment.* Armed services emphasis upon the values of the cumulative record challenges higher education to adopt similar techniques in order to promote student adjustment and coordinate all personnel activities and agencies connected with education and placement.

6. *Encourage educational opportunity.* The Commission emphasized what it felt to be the very democratic selection procedures used by those who had to select personnel for the various wartime college programs. Although its recommendations fell short of suggesting specific alterations in then-current admissions practices or standards, it raised three "debatable questions" about the equalization of educational opportunity: (a) Is it just to deprive students of educational opportunity who possess exceptional and specialized talent but reside in communities lacking publicly supported institutions of higher learning? (b) Should the federal government finance—in addition to the GI educational program and the Army and Navy ROTC programs—a peacetime scholarship system for those possessing potential leadership and high intellect, in order to provide capable personnel in the

vital fields of political leadership and international relations? (c) Should federal funds be made available to the states as a means of expanding facilities for higher education?

While the Commission did not explicitly coin the phrase "the manpower approach," it is clear that a number of the Commission recommendations lead pointedly to the conclusion that manpower planning and forecasting on a national scale are both necessary and desirable. In a final section on National Security Policies, the Commission expresses this notion directly (Grace, 1968, p. 251):

American educational policy should regard the training and education of each individual as having two purposes, the one not necessarily exclusive of the other. The first will consider the individual as entitled to have his inherent abilities and aspirations developed to the utmost; the second will consider the responsibility of the individual as a member of the economic, political, and social organization called the nation. It is the fulfillment of this responsibility whenever the national security is involved that must be recognized and provided for if the strain of the days ahead is to be withstood.

### Assessment

In evaluating the wartime influence, it must be emphasized that in getting ready for the war and living through it, colleges and universities were prepared to accept the direction as phrased by Conant: "Whatever our long-range plans may be for the greater realization of democracy through education, unless the immediate short-range plans for victory are adequate, there will be no free society in America in the future" (Miller and Brooks, 1944, p. 134).

Nevertheless, both during the war and afterward, there were those who thought the war contributed nothing to higher education but an interruption. Fred Kelley, Chief, Division of

Higher Education, U.S. Office of Education, was blunt: "Problems in the field of education do not . . . fall into war versus postwar problems. Most of the problems which now confront institutions of higher education trying to adjust to postwar conditions have their roots in prewar situations. Therefore, this compilation of reports about postwar plans in the colleges and universities can best be characterized by the title 'Higher Education Looks Ahead,' with no direct reference to the influence of the war" (Hollis and Flynt, 1945, p. v).

The assertion made by Kelley was also made by others, but it did not reflect the prevailing evaluation by the higher educational community. The Grace commission analysis was a more accurate mirror of contemporary academic opinion. The potential contributions identified by the commission came to fulfillment in time. These and other innovations in objectives, procedure, and organization, to which reference has already been made, strongly influenced the course of higher education in the 50s and 60s. However, it took time for the wartime experience fully to affect institutional practice. Meanwhile, the overwhelming preoccupation of the immediate postwar years was in providing educational service for returning veterans, a pressurized situation that induced change and reinforced changes that had been born in the war period.

# 4

# Veterans' Return

The enrolment of World War II veterans created the most rapid growth of colleges and universities in the history of higher education. The rate and the time period raised serious doubts as to whether the government had promised more than it could deliver. Failure of the institutions to respond could have had serious social consequences. That higher education was able to marshal resources for the task, whatever the shortcomings in their qualitative performance, is an outstanding record in ingenuity and dedication.

Some may wonder whether a period of prospective limited growth or no growth can learn from the unique experience of a time so completely different. From a description of what happened, anyone may make his own deductions. However, the thoughtful observer will not overlook the willingness to change goals, programs, curriculums, requirements, courses; to create new services in counseling, career placement, and campus activities; and to alter administrative organization and procedures.

The implicit new role gave evidence that higher education held a new priority in public evaluation of its social worth. Consciousness of that new priority was in itself reason enough for renewed effort to fulfill old aspirations as well as new ones. Obviously, new demands created new problems, and new problems bred creative ferment as the debate broadened on how to meet the future.

Organized planning on a national basis for the education of veterans began in the summer of 1942, with a small informal study group called together by the American Council on Education. In July of that year, its membership, with some changes, was designated by President Roosevelt as the Conference on Post-War Readjustment of Civilian and Military Personnel. On November 13, 1942, the president signed the law lowering the draft age to 18 and announced his intention of "the taking of steps to enable young men, whose education has been interrupted, to resume their schooling and afford equal opportunity for the training and education of other young men of ability after their service in the armed forces has come to an end" (Brown, 1949, p. 37). Intense planning followed, within the government, within the higher education community, and among veterans' groups. The American Council on Education had a crucial role in the program formulation finally approved and in its interpretation to the Congress and to the public (Olson, 1974, p. 14).

Although there was no official over-all planning direction, a number of principles emerged in the consensus as to how to proceed, and these were reflected in the final authorizing legislation (Brown, 1949, pp. 38–42):

> The training and education component should not be conceived as primarily a college program. Only 40 percent of the veterans were high school graduates.
>
> Financial assistance to the veteran should be such that his educational opportunity would not be controled by his economic status; at the same time he would be expected to be responsible for some of his living expenses.
>
> Residence location should not be a determining factor in educational opportunity.
>
> Some system for relating institutional capability to individual needs would have to be devised.
>
> Institutions would need assistance in upgrading their physical plants, depleted by wartime retrenchment; in housing accommodations; in conversion of

facilities for temporary use; and in administrative costs.

Two veterans' educational assistance acts passed by Congress made possible an unprecedented federal expenditure in higher education. They were Public Law 346, June 1944, the so-called G.I. Bill, which provided education and training for all military personnel who had served a minimum of 90 days; and earlier, in March 1943, Public Law 16, which expanded the vocational rehabilitation program for veterans with service-connected disabilities. Both had subsequent amendments, but the basic pattern was established (Brown, 1949, p. 40).

The 1944 Bill "provided a minimum of one year of training plus one month for each month of active duty up to a maximum of 48 months. . . . A veteran's full school costs, including tuition, fees, books, and supplies were paid directly by the Veterans Administration, up to a maximum of $500 per school year." A student could be allowed a higher tuition level by reducing his entitlement by one day for each additional $2.10 paid. Student veterans received a monthly subsistence allowance of $50 which was later increased to $65 (1946), then $75 (1948). A statutory ceiling limited benefits if a veteran's monthly income rose above a prescribed figure (which was also increased in a 1948 change).

"Veterans were required to begin training within four years after release from service and were eligible to draw benefits up to nine years after release." Eligibility for full-time benefits required enrolment for a minimum of 12 semester hours in an approved course of instruction, which until 1948 included avocational courses (Educational Testing Service, 1973, pp. 19–21).

While a number of purposes would be served by the legislation, no one purpose can be considered to have been predominantly persuasive in the legislative deliberations—whether the legislation was primarily regarded "as a reward to honor veterans, as a device to replenish the nation's stock of educated citizens, as a means to prevent unemployment, or as a method to help educational institutions" (Olson, 1974, p. 14).

The passage of the legislation without major division or serious opposition probably can be attributed to its multiple plans and purposes for aiding veterans, long a government tradition. Compromise was thus possible and a consensus was achieved after considerable legislative jockeying. The American Legion, "the driving force that made legislation possible" (Olson, 1974, p. 18), obviously was chiefly concerned about veterans and their adjustment to civilian life. The president and others saw the legislation as part of a larger necessity to deal with demobilization on a broad front. The Conference on Post-War Readjustment of Civilian and Military Personnel saw the postwar economy as depressed. "From the war's peak total of 63.5 million jobs, the number would decrease to 57 million jobs. From full employment, 'the number of those unemployed might at one stage in the readjustment period be as large as 8 or 9 million,' with 'the prospects of 3 million persons being unemployed . . . two years after the war.' The report warned that 'once mass unemployment comes into existence, it is not easily dissipated or dissolved.' Wages, hours, prices, moreover, would 'likely return to the levels of 1939–40.' With such a view of the postwar period perhaps it was only natural for the committee to propose and to justify educational programs essentially in a utilitarian light" (Olson, 1974, p. 8) .

Some political defensiveness also underlay the motivation for the legislation. That the Veterans' Bonus had been a disruptive political issue for 15 years after World War I had not been forgotten, nor had the role of unemployed German veterans in the rise of the Nazi party or the political instability in other European countries caused by veterans who could not find jobs. Talk of possible postwar depression was quite common. But the new "rights" and "freedoms" articulated by President Roosevelt provided an appropriate positive setting, however deep-seated the apprehensions about unemployment. The new concept of generous benefits for veterans generally (as contrasted with traditional benefits for the ill and the handicapped) was accepted, and a significant precedent was thereby created for similar action to benefit other veterans and nonveterans in the fifties and sixties.[1] Similarly, the range of benefits provided veterans with World War II service became the standard by which future veterans' benefits programs would be judged.[2]

At the time of the adoption of the legislation, no one anticipated the size of the response. The Army conducted sample surveys in 1943, 1944, and 1945 and the highest estimate of the number of veterans who would return to school *and* college did not exceed 12 percent, with as many as one million who might pursue entry (in both categories) within six months to one year after demobilization. These were the only official surveys, but the conclusion was endorsed by expert opinion. General Frank T. Hines, administrator of the Veterans' Administration, estimated that a total of 700,000 would become college students "distributed over several years," and that existing academic facilities would be adequate. Dr. Earl J. McGrath, then a dean at the University of Buffalo, analyzed the Army's statistics and concluded "that in no academic year will more than 150,000 veterans be full-time students in colleges and universities" (Olson, 1974, pp. 30, 31).

Newspapers did not pay much attention to the subject. Few editorials were written, even when the legislation was under consideration. A special writer for the *Saturday Evening Post* took the theme "G.I.'s Reject Education" and concluded that the G.I. Bill "is a splendid bill, a wonderful bill, with only one conspicuous drawback. The guys aren't buying it." Benjamin

---

[1] Federally funded scholarships for graduate students in certain scientific fields began as early as 1938 and expanded rapidly after the war (Rivlin, 1961, p. 86). Federal funds to assist large numbers of undergraduates were first made broadly available through the loan provisions of the National Defense Education Act of 1958. Direct financial support for students was authorized through the college-level work-study section of the Economic Opportunity Act of 1964. Outright grants of federal funds to undergraduates were incorporated in the Economic Opportunity Grants of the Higher Education Act of 1965.

[2] The legislation establishing the Vietnam Era Veterans' Readjustment Assistance Act of 1972 (Public Law 92–540) mandated a study of the operation of the educational assistance portion of the Act, and specified that the basis of comparison was to be "similar programs of educational assistance that were available to veterans of World War II and the Korean conflict" (Educational Testing Service, 1973, p. III).

Fine of *The New York Times* predicted that the number of veterans might reach a million if unemployment were high (Olson, 1974, pp. 30, 31).

Academic opinion followed generally in the same vein. Sociologist Willard Waller of Columbia University stated in 1944 that veterans would be indifferent to education. President William Mather Lewis of Lafayette College in 1945 told the National Institute of Social Sciences that the number of veterans who would take advantage of the program was being overestimated (Olson, 1974, pp. 28, 31).

The gross underestimation may be traced to the relatively low public interest which did not question the adequacy of the surveys. Publicity was scant because the war news was pre-eminent; when the President signed the legislation, the Allied Invasion of Europe was in its early stage. There had been no attention-getting controversy as the legislation was considered, and the results of the Army surveys were certainly not startling.

As to the surveys, one cannot assess how widespread was the G.I. appreciation of the legislative substance nor the extent to which actual postwar options were a measurable concern. The concept of educational opportunity as a veteran's "benefit" was new. The G.I. had not had previous thought about it or counseling; nor did he have much notion as to what the postwar world would be like.

Factors that later may have influenced veterans to return to the campus were the need for breathing time in making an adjustment to civilian life; the desire for specific career preparation at a time when unemployment possibilities were much discussed; the stimulus received by in-service educational programs; the number of preservice drop-outs or "stop-outs" who had chosen to go into short-term high-paying industrial employment; and the obvious public encouragement to take the education bridge to civilian life.[3]

[3] "Although many thought of the G.I. Bill as an enabling act for college attendance, of the 7,800,000 who received training, 2,200,000 attended college; 3,500,000 went to schools below college level; 1,400,000 took on-the-job training; and 700,000 enrolled in institutional on-farm training." (*Higher Education*, Sept. 1956, *13*, p. 12.) Out of the total expendi-

The miscalculation in the anticipated enrolment count was serious in its impact on the institutions. Whatever planning was done was inadequate and the suddenness and size of the enrolment took on crisis proportions.

The opinions as to what the veterans would be like when they returned were more varied and equally unsubstantiated. Some predicted that they would be angry rebels; others, that they would return as diverse as they went. As students, maturity and purposefulness would be assets, as would social consciousness and experience. However, some feared the military experience would breed restlessness and resistance to authority, while others expected the opposite—indifference and lack of initiative.

On the educational side, Conant would have preferred a more selective program while Hutchins was more harsh, predicting that education would be "demoralized" and the veteran "defrauded." Brown thought the veterans would emphasize vocational education and Stauffer agreed, "The old-style liberal education will be under constant bombardment." There were concerns, too, for campus life. For example, how should institutions deal with student wives and babies? Would veterans and younger undergraduates mix? Was the gap between high school and postwar status too wide for educational success? Should the veterans be segregated (Olson, 1974, pp. 31–33)?

Although the colleges and universities had no knowledge of the massiveness of the undertaking that lay ahead and could not therefore plan for the load, they did have some practice with smaller numbers of veterans before demobilization. Some veterans came to the campus under the Public Law 16 as soon as it was approved in March 1943. No special difficulties arose because the law followed the practices of the rehabilitation program which had been initiated after World War I, with application to civilians in later years. Others entered in 1944–45 under the G.I. Bill; in fact, some 88,000 by November 1945.

Most institutions created postwar planning committees soon after the start of the war. With the definition and develop-

---

ture $14.5 billion (*Higher Education,* Sept. 1956, *13,* p. 12) about $5.5 billion was for the higher education portion (Olson, 1974, p. 59).

ment of the program for veterans' education, special veterans' committees became common either in connection with the work of the general planning committee or separately. The committees were usually staffed by a director of veterans' affairs who also had responsibility for veterans' counseling. Thus the institutional machinery for gathering information, for communication, and for planning was generally set up by 1945. At the national level, the American Council on Education and other associations of institutions established offices for special service regarding veterans' affairs, enabling institutions to share experiences quickly and effectively. However, neither national advisory bodies nor inexperienced institutional planners could anticipate the welter and variety of needs that would characterize the day by day administrative and instructional operations. Only actual experience and creative response "on the firing line" could bring the necessary adjustments.

By consensus, the institutions approached the veterans as students rather than as veterans, but acknowledged the importance of flexibility in meeting special needs as they arose. In general, veterans were given preference in admissions and admitted by examination if high school had not been completed. In most institutions, credit was allowed for military education and certain kinds of other military experience, in accordance with an elaborate and comprehensive guide developed by the American Council on Education. Calendars were altered for the convenience of the veterans, short courses were established for interim periods, and refresher courses were offered. Exceptions were made in departmental requirements and sometimes in degree requirements. Rigidities were minimized and the educational needs of the individual became a first concern. Student personnel work, which previously had received little academic support, was transformed from monitoring student life to a professional service, a trend that survived and was the basis for later developments in this field.

The acceleration of veteran enrolments began in February 1946, when 125,000 new veterans registered. By fall, over a million crowded the campuses. "Ten years later, when the last student had received his last check, the V.A. . . . counted 2,232,-

000 veterans who had attended college under the G.I. Bill. . . . By the fall of 1947, at the peak of veteran enrolment, the number of males registered and the percentage of persons 18–20 years old enroled in colleges had more than doubled the prewar records; total college enrolment, greater by over a million, had climbed by 75 percent. For three years the majority of all male students were veterans" (Olson, 1974, p. 43) .

The distribution by institutions varied greatly, of course. Prominent institutions were most popular. Some regional and limited program colleges and universities were the last to be chosen. Rutgers, for example, more than doubled its prewar peak as did many others. Yet "at the opening session of the Association of American Colleges Conference in January 1946, educators reported that the smaller liberal arts colleges still had room for 250,000 veterans. . . . Forty-one percent of all veterans that spring registered at 38 institutions, with the remaining 59 scattered among 712 other fully accredited schools" (Olson, 1974, p. 45). Eventually, some two thousand institutions were involved.

The educational performance of veterans was almost as unanticipated and as impressive as the number of enrolments. The most extensive survey of the educational achievement of the veterans concluded that they tended to have higher grades in relation to their academic ability than nonveteran students (Frederiksen and Schrader, 1951, p. 6) . The achievement difference was not large but the fact was unexpected. The conclusion of the survey was widely supported by individual testimony, with emphasis on the qualities assumed to be influential in the academic outcome. At the University of Pennsylvania, the director of the Veterans Advisory Council stated that "the veteran is acknowledged to be serious, time conscious, industrious, and capable." A University of Minnesota administrator called veterans "assertive, positive, and active." A *Fortune* magazine survey stated that the national class of 1949, with 70 percent veterans, was "the best, . . . the most mature, . . . the most responsible, . . . and the most self-disciplined group" of college students in history. Conant of Harvard said that the veterans were "the most mature and promising students Harvard has ever had" (Olson, 1974, p. 49) . Similar complimentary judgments were made about the ease with which the veterans adjusted to civilian and campus life.

The veterans were good copy for journalists and good subjects for research. These students responded willingly to inquiries and were accessible as a group. The evaluators may never know for sure the reasons for the academic success of the veterans, beyond the generally accepted premise that they were composed of a greater proportion of highly motivated people than would normally be attracted to college. But whatever the cause, the result was a positive influence on the public appraisal of the college experience.

An account of the ways and means by which institutions managed "the deluge" is a separate story, full of drama and human interest and reflecting resourcefulness, imagination, ingenuity, and dedicated response to a public responsibility and professional opportunity. Most educators and observers appreciate that the task was unique and that it would last for less than a decade, but that realization did not lessen the enormity of the administrative and educational problems. Snafus were common and the inadequacies obvious. There simply were not enough beds, teachers, classrooms, and laboratories; not enough equipment, libraries, offices, food service centers, and ordinary services. The results were overcrowding, inconveniences, and countless irritations. Yet the experience came off with good spirit in nearly all quarters, with remarkable educational results, and few regrets on the part of the institutions or the veterans. The latter were remarkably patient and understanding, seeming to sense the emergency nature of their predicament and the tremendous effort on their behalf. They realized, too, that conditions could not be much improved in their time. A mood of gratitude for being back and assisted with a productive purpose prevailed.

Housing was a major difficulty. The nation had a housing shortage of immense proportions, occasioned by lack of construction and upkeep during the war years. Needs of the veterans on and off campus simply made a bad situation worse. The federal government acted quickly with housing assistance by contributing and moving temporary buildings from camps and other surplus areas; by supplying funds for conversion of barracks, duplexes, and local improvisations; and by encouraging the use of federal facilities near campuses. Similar aid was extended for academic space. Trailer towns and "vetsvilles" became common (and lasted far beyond their intended use!). State and local governments also rallied cooperatively with authorizations and funds.

The mood at the federal level was one of full cooperation. Although the Veterans Administration was officially the chief administrator, it was as nonrestrictive as possible—almost too much so, in some instances, as petty graft, overstaffing, and other irregularities were revealed in later audits, particularly in the noncollegiate segments of the program. At the higher education level, the irregularities were minor in effect and in proportion to the size of the operation. The fear of federal control of education was dissipated and liaison with the Congress, the Federal Housing Administration, the Federal Security Agency, the Office of Education, and the educational associations was surprisingly effective.

Although the G.I. Bill provided many benefits for veterans beyond those pertaining to higher education, and although still other benefits were the subject of additional legislation, the action pertaining to education was by far the most significant. It was representative of the national attitude toward veterans and reflected widespread concerns about demobilization and the postwar future.

Planning started with an uneasiness that allowed a columnist for *The New Republic* to claim that demobilization would be "a Pearl Harbor of Peace." Instead, a professional historian was able to say in 1969, "The education benefits helped spur the development of America's schools and colleges; they also gave to the participating men and women opportunities that they might otherwise have missed; a generation of youth had reaped a rich harvest" (Ross, 1969, pp. 34, 28). Ross concluded that the veterans' total benefits "have contributed to making the Ulysses of World War II more happy for having survived than bitter for having served. It is reasonable to suggest that these benefits have helped Americans avoid repetition of ugly veteran-civilian clashes. The federal government, in giving aid liberally to nondisabled veterans in such an unprecedented fashion, had established an important principle: Ulysses deserves a helping hand not only to get him to Troy, but to ease him back into life in Ithaca" (1969, pp. 290–291).

Although writing about the experiences of the veterans and of the institutions with the G.I. Bill program is abundant, research on the subsequent impact on the higher education system is scanty. However, from the observations of others and from my own participation in the administration of G.I. programs, I mark a number of significant changes occasioned by the veterans' return:

(1) Higher education clearly became a significant means to a national end for the policymakers—even for those whose interest was limited to veterans' readjustment and for those who were primarily concerned about preventing or alleviating unemployment and other negative economic conditions. The perception of higher education as a "benefit" in the fulfilment of both objectives, with the concept overwhelmingly supported by the public, was a tremendous psychological lift for the educational system—a system that had been battered by the Depression and by the indifference in the early years of war preparation.

(2) The nonveteran youth of the nation were quick to note the new priority for higher education. They, their families, and their counselors were prompted to consider higher education for the same reasons as veterans—improved career options and mobility.

(3) Those who were concerned with the enlargement of educational opportunity, particularly for the economically deprived and young people disadvantaged in other ways, were given a national precedent for the value and feasibility of federal assistance.

(4) Aid to students generally emerged, as it had in the Depression, as an appropriate way for the federal government to be involved in higher education with a minimum of federal control. It is reasonable to assume that the precedents were influential in the adoption of the student assistance features of the

National Defense Education Act and the Higher Education Act of 1965.

(5) The public image of the veteran as a good student, reliable, mature, and well motivated, carried over into the public evaluation of college students generally. This regard persisted in the revival of the fifties and early sixties, supported by the growth of graduate work and professional education, and lasted until the late sixties, ending with the period of campus violence and politicization.

(6) The new status of higher education broadened the appeal of academic careers for increasing numbers of highly qualified young people.

(7) The temporary acquisition of off-campus sites for "surplus" enrolments at a number of institutions served as beginnings for permanent new campuses in state systems, as foundations for new community colleges, and as later authorized permanent branches. The Chicago Circle campus at the University of Illinois had its origin in a Chicago warehouse on Navy Pier, opened to serve G.I.s in the area. A community college succeeded the University of Illinois installation at Danville. Impetus for organization of the State University of New York was heightened by the experience with veterans at the hastily organized Associated Colleges of Upper New York State (Olson, 1974, p. 71). Similar experiences occurred in Pennsylvania, Indiana, and many other states. Such developments as satellite centers reinforced the notion that all education does not have to take place on a central campus. This led not only to the creation of new institutions but modified the strong preconceptions of the importance of single-site learning that had dominated higher education in the past. Current offshoots of that change are cluster colleges, multicampus systems, and open institutions. The origins of extension activity are earlier, but the postwar experience made it more acceptable and encouraged new forms.

(8) The tone of campus life was changed. Undergraduate discipline systems were altered. The married student came to stay. In loco parentis did not disappear for another decade, but a break-through was made that kept widening with succeeding

years. Student personnel work grew in importance. The exceptions to curricular rigidities for veterans made easier the adoption of permanent revisions in educational practice. Change was encouraged.

(9) Many other internal practices, policies, and services were initiated that would become permanent. The new flexibility in admissions would remain. Many previously experimental nontraditional arrangements had new acceptance and continued in force—correspondence instruction, short courses, tutorial clinics, and remedial courses. Student counseling expanded. Career preparation had new interest and influenced college curriculums as well as over-all objectives of some institutions. This emphasis also encouraged public community college development and that of post-high school proprietary schools. Urban universities earned renewed attention because of their accessibility and their capability for improvisation in cooperation with city agencies. Year-round schooling became popular and induced change in academic calendars and offerings. Student life took on adult perspectives in many ways. New relationships with community agencies for instruction and service were forged. The part-time teacher from professional life became a fixture in many institutions. These and similar developments should have the attention of the educational historian in the analysis of change and adaptation in higher education.

With the return of the veterans, higher education passed through another crisis. The benefits to the veterans and to the nation were obvious. The benefits to higher education were also numerous, if less visible. They came not because of enrolment growth, but because a clearly understood public objective was successfully attained, an objective widely acknowledged to be of importance not only to those directly involved but to the economic and social welfare of the nation. The new public esteem for higher education would be a continuing asset of unmeasured value, psychologically and pragmatically.

# 5

## New Concepts and Emerging Goals

As higher education emerged from World War II, the academic community had the feeling that colleges and universities had a new importance in national affairs. Academic men of science had been heavily involved in bringing about the harnessing of atomic energy. Many faculty members had served in important wartime posts for the government and for business, industry, and civic affairs related to the war effort (Handlin and Handlin, 1970, pp. 74–75). The campuses had been given recognition as an important segment of war training, both for military and homefront employment. Higher education as an instrument of national policy in the postwar demobilization was a psychological lift and was taken as a portent of a new place for higher education among national priorities. Widespread approbation of higher education in view of its response to the veterans' needs reinforced the mood. The expansive view of future potential in the report of the President's Commission (1947) made clear that there was important work to do, and one could infer that such an analysis would be recognized and its recommendations implemented.

The new mood induced new ideas. The experience in war training and in adjusting to veterans' needs revealed weaknesses in the system and bred new ideas and approaches. In 1950, O. C. Carmichael, President of the Carnegie Foundation for the Advancement of Teaching, wrote: "At no time in the history of this country has there been so much ferment and stir about the ends and means of education. . . . The questions have not yet been answered, but the fact that they are being asked with such persistence and by so many is the most encouraging sign of our times" (cited in *School and Society,* December 16, 1950, *72,* p. 392).

It was noted earlier that postwar planning committees were commonly created within institutions early in the war period and that these groups were looking at many long-standing issues. The committees were a bridge from the prewar debates on the desirability of restructuring higher education, particularly dealing with the growing diversity of the larger student body. As the war ended, the committees faced a new setting, however. They had to consider what the postwar world would be like—prosperous or depressed; enrolment growing or declining; the national mood isolationist or international; resources to remedy deficits in plants, personnel, and programs as well as resources for innovations. The committees did not know whether the needs of higher education would have a priority below other reconversion interests in public works, industrial development, and commerce (Russell, 1944, 1945).

The institutional planning groups were not alone. State associations of colleges and universities grew in number and in concern for cooperative planning; governors' committees were established and included education in their purview; and national associations of the professions became active in educational planning. Similar activity characterized every other segment of American life. As early as 1944, the Council of State Governments indicated that $13 billion would be needed for 60,000 state and local public works projects (Hollis and Flynt, 1945, pp. 18–19). Some of the recommendations for higher education were also very specific. The prewar foreign student enrolment of 10,000 was estimated to grow to 50,000 and would require special handling. The National Association of Housing Officials wanted more highly trained recruits. The National Association of Broadcasters outlined an instructional guide for programs in radio journalism. Expansion of adult education was on all lists of educational recommendations. Educational topics state authorities mentioned most frequently were high school and college articulation, terminal education, and increased effectiveness in teacher education (Hollis and Flynt, 1945, pp. 14–27).

For higher education, the focal point of much of the discussion were the recommendations of the President's Commission on Higher Education, published in six small volumes during the period from December 1947 to February 1948 under the general title *Higher Education for American Democracy.*[1]

The Commission, appointed in July 1946, consisted of 28 members under the chairmanship of George F. Zook, then President of the American Council on Education. The main (and at the time startling) thrust of the report was the elimination of all barriers to educational opportunity, so that "every citizen, youth, and adult is enabled and encouraged to carry his education, formal and informal, as far as his native capacities permit (President's Commission on Higher Education, 1947, *1*, p. 101). The recommendation was based on the conviction that "at least 49 percent of our population has the mental ability to complete 14 years of schooling," while "at least 32 percent of our population has the mental ability to complete an advanced liberal or specialized professional education" (President's Commission on Higher Education, 1947, *1,* p. 41). The commission believed that a majority of people with abilities at these levels would desire higher education but were deprived of opportunities by economic restraints and by racial, religious, and geographical considerations.

To accomplish its goals, the commission recommended

---

[1] The individual volumes were entitled 1. Establishing the Goals; 2. Equalizing and Expanding Individual Opportunity; 3. Organizing Higher Education; 4. Staffing Higher Education; 5. Financing Higher Education; and 6. Resource Data. For summary, see Technical Note C in the Final Report of the Carnegie Commission on Higher Education, *Priorities for Action,* New York: McGraw Hill, 1973b, pp. 130–138.

doubling enrolments by 1960, development of community colleges, federal scholarships and fellowships, federal aid for general purposes and for physical plant in public institutions, and legislation to prevent religious and racial discrimination.

The Commission pointed to new social needs over and beyond the needs of the individual to justify the nature and scope of its recommendations (President's Commission on Higher Education, 1947, *1*, p. 2) :

> *Trained manpower.* "Science and invention have diversified natural resources, have multiplied new devices and techniques of production. . . . New skills and greater maturity are required of youth as they enter upon their adult roles."
>
> *Unity in diversity.* "Of and among . . . diversities our free society seeks to create dynamic unity. Where there is . . . tension, we undertake to effect democratic reconciliation."
>
> *World knowledge.* "The Nation's traditional isolationism has been displaced by a new sense of responsibility in world affairs. . . . America's role . . . requires of our citizens a knowledge of other peoples —of their political and economic systems, their social and cultural institutions—such as has not hitherto been so urgent."
>
> *The atomic age* "has intensified the uncertainties of the future . . . has deepened and broadened the responsibilities of higher education for anticipating and preparing for the social and economic changes that will come with the application of atomic energy to industrial use."

The commission obviously felt that it was speaking at a time of crisis. The atomic bomb threatened possible world obliteration, but the same power had positive uses for the betterment of mankind. The direction of its use would be determined by "Education for a fuller realization of democracy in every phase of living . . . for international understanding and cooperation . . . for the application of creative imagination and trained intelligence to the solution of social problems and to the administration of public affairs" (President's Commission on Higher Education, 1947, *1*, p. 8).

The general goal of the report—to expand educational opportunity toward mass higher education—was widely endorsed, although not without dissent. (It is interesting to speculate about how much this favorable reaction was induced by the popularity of the higher education provisions of the G.I. Bill.) But the debate on "ways and means" and appropriate limitations was widespread and centered on feasibility, desirability of educating so many, the content of higher education for diverse groups, and federal relationships.

The report was the first comprehensive rationale for mass higher education to be presented under the auspices of a government appointed group, although the subject was not new and the trend lines had been obvious. Further, the commission was regarded as a source of potential influence on national policy formulation. This combination invited confrontation and the critics responded vigorously, sometimes savagely.

Stylistically, the report was criticized for vagueness, overgeneralization, philosophical ambiguity, and some inconsistency. A bitter assault came from Hutchins (1952, p. 81), who characterized the report as "confused, confusing, and contradictory. It has something for everybody. It is generous, ignoble, bold, timid, naive, and optimistic. It is filled with the spirit of universal brotherhood and the sense of American superiority. It has great faith in money. It has great faith in courses. It is antihumanistic and anti-intellectual. It is confident that vices can be turned into virtues by making them larger. Its heart is in the right place; its head does not work very well. Every cliché and every slogan of contemporary educational discussion appear once more. Much of the report reads like a Fourth-of-July oration in pedagoguese. It skirts the edge of illiteracy, and sometimes falls over the brink. And, when the battle has ended, the field is strewn with the corpses of the straw men the Commission has slain."

Had Hutchins been right in this assessment, the report would not have merited his attention; nor would it have aroused the debate that ensued or been worthy of its critics. After these verbal pyrotechnics, Hutchins concedes "that the Commission is right about many things." He lists particularly the recommendation on eliminating barriers to educational opportunity and stressing adult education, and acknowledges that "the Commission is right on many other matters with which it deals more briefly" (1952, p. 82).

Hutchins saw correctly that the core of the report was its emphasis on diversity—among students, curricula, and objectives—and the need to interrelate these elements appropriately, whereas he believed that "the primary aim of higher education is the development of intellectual power" (1952, p. 86). Disagreement on organization, curriculum, quality, scope followed naturally from these two conflicting premises.

Forthright objection to certain features of the report came from some educators who spoke from a "private higher education" point of view. Hollinshead, then President of Coe College, feared that the recommendations of the Commission, if carried out, would "swamp" the colleges and universities not supported by the state. Hollinshead declared that the "present and future deluge of taxpayers' money going to the support of public colleges" posed a threat that should be the basis of an appeal "to our fellow-Americans" (1952, p. 90). This argument brought into the open again the long-standing public-private division in the higher education community. A notable earlier instance was the opposition of some private college presidents to the proposed Land-Grant legislation in 1860. The Commission Report opened old sores that would continue to fester as further federal assistance became an issue.

Two commission members, private college educators, dissented from the report: Frederick G. Hochwalt, director, Department of Education, National Catholic Welfare Conference, and Martin R. P. McGuire, dean of the Graduate School of Arts and Sciences, Catholic University of America. These members dissented because federal funds for capital outlay and current expenditures would be restricted "for use in publicly controlled institutions of higher education only." They objected to the theory that "public control" rather than "service to the public" should be the eligibility criterion for public funds. These educators outlined the possible negative consequences of such a policy (President's Commission on Higher Education, 1947, *5*, pp. 65–68).

Some private college leaders objected to federal aid to any institutions, private or public. Positions on this issue were divided within the public institution constituency as well as between the two sectors. Ten years later the question was debated on the senate floor of the National Association of State Universities and Land-Grant Colleges, and the question was not settled until federal legislation was adopted, without the restriction, and sustained in the courts. The forum for similar debate has now moved to the state level, where state aid for private institutions has been adopted in a number of instances and the concept appears to be gaining in acceptance.

Another main center of discussion was the quantitative objectives of the report: By 1960, 4,600,000 young people "should be in nonprofit institutions for education beyond the traditional twelfth grade. Of this total number, 2,500,000 should be in the thirteenth and fourteenth grades (junior college level); 1,500,000 in the fifteenth and sixteenth grades (senior college level); and 600,000 in graduate and professional schools beyond the first degree" (President's Commission on Higher Education, 1947, *1*, p. 39). The enrolment at the beginning of 1948 was 2,408,000.

Some educators were apprehensive about the economic and social impact of such numbers in so short a time. Harris of Harvard wrote of "Millions of B.A.'s But No Jobs." "How would a college-graduate population five times as large as in 1932 react to a severe depression and mass unemployment? Some of the results can be anticipated. Frustration. Anti-intellectualism. The bolstering of revolutionary forces by millions of college graduates who had hoped to be executives, college teachers, physicians and lawyers. Bumper crops of new graduates thrown into an economy unprepared to absorb them would certainly bring with them a bumper crop of disillusionment"

(1952, p. 71). Harris noted "the contributions of the disappointed intellectuals to the rise of fascism in Europe."

Henderson (1952, p. 72), a member of the commission, advised against planning on a Depression base. He believed that new numbers of graduates would be absorbed into the employment market in nontraditional ways if students were influenced to think about education in nonvocational terms and if attention were given to the need for trained brainpower in nontraditional areas of employment. New vocational tracks requiring post-high school education were in the making, Henderson said, and manpower surpluses have a way of self-correcting maldistribution by fields if there is adequate advance information.

Charles Luckman, then head of Lever Brothers, was even more expansive: "Is it not about time for us to make another historic declaration of war—this time on Ignorance?" (quoted in *Ferment in Education,* 1948, p. 79).

But could such a system of postsecondary education be financed? The President's Commission on Higher Education (1947, 5, p. 1) believed that millions of additional funds, to be supplied by the federal government, would be adequate (excluding capital outlay). The total cost for financing higher education, if all of the Commission's recommendations were adopted, would be $2,587,000,000; $1,548,000,000 would be shared by the state and federal governments and the remainder divided among student fees, local government, and philanthropy. On feasibility, the commission related the costs to Gross National Product. Pointing out that the ratio of current educational expenditures to GNP had slipped from .63 percent in 1932 to .47 percent in 1947, the report held that a reversal of that trend to underwrite an achievement of 1.19 percent by 1960 (1.50 percent if needed capital outlay were included) would not be an unreasonable investment in higher education (President's Commission on Higher Education, 1947, 5, p. 26).

On curriculum, it was to be expected that general education would have the attention of a commission recommending mass higher education as a means of advancing democracy. The search for a "modern equivalent" of the classical tradition began with an effort to balance the land-grant emphasis on career education and the subsequent development of specialization in disciplines and professional studies. "General education" became a label to identify courses and programs designed to bring order to what some thought was educational chaos. The cluster of survey courses, which in most places constituted the required elements in the degree program, did not appear to many to be the sought-after unifying or integrating educational experience that would assure "the continuance of the liberal and humane tradition" (Conant, 1970, p. 368).

In 1919, Columbia University "devised a course on contemporary civilization whose purpose was to define the 'intellectual and spiritual tradition that a man must experience and understand if he is to be called educated.' The College at the University of Chicago made a still more ambitious effort to structure undergraduate teaching so that it would be unfettered by the boundaries of conventional departments and disciplines" (Handlin and Handlin, 1970, pp. 78–79). The Harvard Report adopted in 1945 was a major effort, widely influencial although designed for Harvard College.

The key term continued to mean different things to different people and the commission recommendations on the subject were no exception. "General education," said the President's Commission on Higher Education (1947, *1,* p. 49), "is the term that has come to be accepted for those phases of nonspecialized and nonvocational learning which should be the common experience of all educated men and women. General education should give to the student the values, attitudes, knowledge, and skills that will equip him to live rightly and well in a free society. . . . But the knowledge and understanding which general education aims to secure, whether drawn from the past or from a living present, are not to be regarded as ends in themselves. They are means to a more abundant personal life and a stronger, freer social order." The commission perceived the difference between general education and liberal education to be one of degree, not of kind. But the Commission on Liberal Education of the Association of American Colleges came to the conclusion that the concepts and distinctions of the presidential commission, "not only betray a basic confusion upon what constitutes general and what liberal education, but will be construed as an attack upon liberal education as such" (Farrell, 1952, p. 101).

The confusion in interpretation arose partly from a lack of agreement on definition, partly from differences in proposed institutional applications of general concepts, and partly from differences in emphasis.[2] Many interpreted the intent of the President's Commission as giving primacy to the social role of higher education as compared with the intellectual development of the individual, and to education in terms of democracy rather than in terms of the person. In stressing the point, critics were apprehensive about the secularization of higher education, the dilution of quality through mass higher education, statism in finance and control, and dominance by utilitarianism. In many instances critics were interpreting their fears as to what was meant rather than what was said (McConnell, 1952, pp. 106–115), and those critics found it difficult to accept the commentary on general education at face value.

The recommendations on general education dealt with a subject that had its roots in nearly a century of deliberation, experimentation, and adaptation. Its new priority was a postwar phenomenon, however. In contrast, another subject of the Commission's report was also a postwar development, but without a background in educational history: "Toward International Understanding and Cooperation" (President's Commission on Higher Education, 1947, *1*, pp. 14–20). It was expressed under the headings Defense of Peace, Preparation for World Citizenship, and Instruments of International Cooperation.

Related to this theme was the difficulty experienced by foreign students in seeking admission to overcrowded campuses where veterans had priority. The problem was enlarged because of the anticipated additional numbers from war-

---

[2] The confusions persist. Pifer (1972, p. 14) calls the content of undergraduate education "one of the most difficult and most central issues in higher education today" and indicates that this is regarded by many as the "disaster area" of liberal education.

ravaged countries (Brown, 1946, p. 107). However, the context was broader—the concept that exchange of students "is a great opportunity to contribute to intercultural understanding and international peace" (Brown, 1946, p. 109).

That higher education should respond to such an opportunity in ways other than through exchange of students was a commission conviction and the recommendations bear upon curriculum, courses, research, and campus life. A continuing concern should be the development of ways and means to "help our own citizens as well as other peoples to move from the provincial and insular mind to the international mind. . . . This will involve . . . the study of all aspects of international affairs." World thinking must replace both national and regional provincialism "to fit ourselves for the world leadership that has fallen to America in this crucial moment of history" (President's Commission on Higher Education, 1947, *1*, pp. 15, 17). Some also saw international exchange as a way to enhance appreciation for American democracy. The point subsequently came in for sharp criticism, however, with the publication of *The Ugly American*.

Few people took issue with the recommendations of the commission on international education, although there would be skirmishes on this front in the fifties as a result of the Cold War. With government and foundation help, area studies, A.I.D. contracts, large foreign student constituencies, and study abroad programs gradually became common features of higher education as did research in international history, culture, politics, and economics. But the widely acclaimed International Education Act of 1968 remains to be funded and the potential described in the 1948 commission report is still unfulfilled.

Approximately a year after the final report of the President's Commission appeared, the Commission on Financing Higher Education was created by the Association of American Universities. The new commission was funded by the Rockefeller Foundation and the Carnegie Corporation, and included 12 members. Millett, then professor of public administration at Columbia University, was chosen as executive director and made responsible for drafting the report of the commission.

Millett also supervised supporting studies and the staff report *Financing Higher Education in the United States.* The commission stated that its main purpose was "to provide a general view of the status of higher education in American culture, its economic problems, and the choices for future financial development" (1952, p. xi). The report included recommendations for action.

Although the central interest of the Commission on Financing Higher Education was, as its name suggests, on finance, its general report was entitled *Nature and Needs of Higher Education.* Thus, the commentary overlaps considerably with the earlier President's Commission on Higher Education. Both tied their recommendations on economic problems and sources of support to their concept of "diversity as the key to freedom" and analyzed the functions of higher education in societal relationships.

On a number of issues the two commissions ran parallel but on some they were sharply divergent. Henderson (1953, p. 195) set down some contrasting paragraphs from the two reports:

> 1-A. American society requires two interrelated but fundamentally different kinds of education. One is common schooling. Its goal is the steady improvement in the literacy and social competence of the individual. The public primary and secondary school is the chief instrument of this purpose, although it has always been accompanied and sometimes stimulated by the private school. The other education goal is the development of the intellectual capacities of those possessing unusual talent. This is the special province of higher education (Commission on Financing Higher Education, 1952, pp. 12–13).
>
> 1-B. American colleges and universities must envision a much larger role for higher education in the national life. They can no longer consider themselves merely the instrument for producing an intellectual elite. They must become the means by which

every citizen, youth, and adult is enabled and encouraged to carry his education, formal and informal, as far as his native capacities permit (President's Commission on Higher Education, 1947, *1*, p. 101).

2-A. We believe higher education should accept as its first concern the education of those young people who fall approximately within the top 25 percent in intellectual capacity (Commission on Financing Higher Education, 1952, p. 48).

2-B. At least 49 percent of our population has the mental ability to complete 14 years of schooling with a curriculum of general and vocational studies that should lead either to gainful employment or to further study at a more advanced level. At least 32 percent of our population has the mental ability to complete an advanced liberal or specialized professional education (President's Commission on Higher Education, 1947, vol. *1*, p. 41).

3-A. The term "adult education" designates a clientele, not a function (Millett, 1952, p. 12).

3-B. The colleges and universities should elevate adult education to a position of equal importance with any other of their functions. . . . Adult education in the past has been too inflexible, much too bound by traditional notions of proper educational procedures. Extension activities for years have been stultified by the idea that adult education consists merely of the transmission to mature people of campus courses developed to meet the needs of adolescents (President's Commission on Higher Education, 1947, *1*, p. 97, 98).

4-A. Certainly it would seem a mistake to assume that student charges at public universities can or should take the place of generous appropriations by state legislatures. Student charges can be a desirable and useful supplement, especially in a period of stringency in state public finances (Millett, 1952, p. 387). . . .

It appears to be relatively simple today for many young men to earn a substantial part of the cost of higher education, even as they have done in the past (Millett, 1952, p. 392).

4-B. In addition to the recommendation that student fees be eliminated for grades 13 and 14 in publicly controlled institutions of higher education, this Commission recommends that the fees for the upper grades in such institutions be rolled back at the earliest opportunity to the level prevailing in 1939 (President's Commission on Higher Education, 1947, 5, p. 35). . . .

Institutions under private control also must avoid excessive fees if their contribution to higher education is to be of greater benefit. While most of these institutions of necessity must depend heavily upon fees as a source of financial support, they cannot be unaware at all times of the effect which high fees may have in limiting the advantages of their services largely to students from families in the upper income brackets (President's Commission on Higher Education, 1947, 2, p. 51).

5-A. Nevertheless, after giving due weight to all these considerations this Commission has reached the unanimous conclusion that we as a nation should call a halt at this time to the introduction of new programs of direct federal aid to colleges and universities. We also believe it undesirable for the government to expand the scope of its scholarship aid to individual students (Commission on Financing Higher Education, 1952, pp. 157–158).

5-B. The time has come for America to develop a sound pattern of continuing federal support for higher education (President's Commission on Higher Education, 1947, 5, p. 54). . . .

The inadequacy of existing funds for scholarships and fellowships makes a national program imperative if higher education is to fulfill its responsibility to the individual, to the nation and to the world (President's Commission on Higher Education, 1947, 2, p. 51).

Many other differences may be identified. This might be anticipated in a comparison of two reports proceeding on different tracks, even though the destination was agreed upon— the public necessity for a strengthened and enlarged system of higher education. The approach of the first commission was expansive and comprehensive in its social point of view; the approach of the second commission could be called moderate, if not conservative, and probably more realistic as to what might be accomplished.

The two reports are valuable to those people interested in the history of higher education because the reports identify a large number of subjects that dominated educational discussion at that time. Further, the analysis of data was scholarly in both instances and the data-gathering impressive in scope and organization. Many of the recommendations found their way into action; many others remain on the agenda for the seventies. The setting has changed but the current conditions are reminiscent of the era immediately following World War II, and many of the problems then being discussed remain to be resolved. (Some of the farsighted topics that were reinforced by both reports or related commentary were an enlarged concept of public service by colleges and universities, special programs for the gifted, the need for peacetime manpower policies, and the need for more and better trained teachers.)

The direct influence of the two reports is difficult to assess. Many believe that recommendations of task forces and study groups are an exercise in futility. Those who expect immediate results and results in the form recommended are usually disappointed. In studying the development of higher education for more than 20 years, however, one is impressed with the extent to which the positions of these two study groups are reflected in legislation, national and state policy, public attitudes, and institutional behavior. This fact reinforces the belief that consensus in governance can be influenced by public debate and discussion, which can be better informed by good professional staff work and by expert opinion, however diverse. Otherwise, policy formulation may be unduly influenced by propaganda, prejudice, and narrow interest. These have their place and may be useful in inducing public discussion as long as the results of scholarship, expertise, and objective analysis are also available for contribution to wise reconciliation of differing viewpoints and to innovative problem-solving.

It becomes increasingly clear, therefore, that through this educational ferment of the early postwar years one may trace the threads of continuity to the present—threads knotted or reinforced, as fate would have it, by the events and forces of the fifties and sixties.

# 6

## Uncertainty During Cold War

In January 1951, Arthur Adams, the president of the American Council on Education, opened an annual conference with these words: "Today, we are afflicted with uncertainty—uncertainty now and uncertainty with respect to the days, months, and years ahead. The current general attitude seems to be a rather grudging acceptance of the inevitable. The Kremlin makes a move, and we counter it, not because we want to, but because we must" (Brown, 1951, p. 5).

Walters (1951, p. 32), president of the University of Cincinnati, addressing the 1951 annual conference of AAUP, reflected the prevailing mood of the country and the academic community. He identified two assumptions that underlay higher education planning "for the present and for the long run." First, "the challenge of Soviet Communism does in fact constitute a national emergency, a real and present danger." Second, "military strength becomes an indispensable resource" in a potential conflict that Stalin had called "inevitable."

The uncertainty of higher education during the fifties was largely fallout from the Cold War. The anti-Communist stance of the nation called for increased defense expenditures and affected the economy. Inflation was on the rise, partly caused by financing armaments and other aid to allies. The partial mobilization raised questions about manpower policy, including the probable continuation of Selective Service and the possibility of universal military training. The debate affected student choice as to college attendance and reduced the capability of institutions to anticipate future enrolment. The situation seriously affected the morale of college and university personnel, not only through the influence upon finance and mission, but in the harassment that came with the McCarthy confrontations and the little McCarthy committees at the state level; in unfair attacks on the loyalty of teachers, textbooks, and student groups; in loyalty oaths, with all their implications; and in vicious heresy-hunting. Pressures from economy drives were an additional discouragement.

Living now in a time of new global strategies, of detente, and of a growing recognition that world problems affect the well-being of each nation, we have difficulty understanding public acceptance in the fifties of the urgent necessity for military defenses for possible conflict with the Soviet Union, and the general feeling of immediate danger. The aggression in Austria and Poland, the fall of China to a Communist government, the belligerence of Soviet spokesmen, Communist domination of eastern Europe, the confusion in Asia and the Middle East seemed to indicate a Third World War in the near future. Few doubts were raised about the necessity for a garrison state, for military manpower as a first priority, and for all sectors of the economy to tailor their programs to the national defense requirements. Russian development of the atomic bomb and the military action in Korea and Berlin merely underscored the developing tensions.

A report jointly sponsored by the Educational Policies Commission and the American Council on Education (1951, p. 1) stated that world war was not inevitable but further declared that "A strongly rearmed West will be necessary for the security of the world until such time as other methods of maintaining peace are dependable and effective. . . . All this means an American economy geared for an indefinite period to a partial mobilization basis."

In this setting, the subject most immediately troublesome

to colleges and universities was the inability to plan for enrolments. As the veterans left the campuses, who would take their places? Veteran enrolment dropped from 1,122,738 in 1947 to 388,747 in 1951, and the downward trend would continue (Millett, 1952, pp. 68–70). What proportion of high school graduates would enter college? The number of males becoming 18 annually would remain fairly stable until 1956, and then rise slowly (Educational Policies Commission and others, 1951, p. 42). Would colleges and universities continue to attract the traditional 20 percent of high school graduates, or would the number be increased by a federal student aid plan? What would be the impact of junior college enrolment upon the senior institutions, even should the total student number increase? To what extent would rising costs affect student ability to enrol? What would be the effect of new military policies as to the induction of young men?

Six-month military training for all 18-year-old men, to be followed by part-time reserve training, was seriously debated. This arrangement would have required minimum adjustment for the institutions, but no one knew whether it would be workable in the "half-war" situation. The two-year draft under Selective Service finally prevailed, but with service postponed for many college enrolees. The postponements were a constant source of argument and irritation, and the threat of a change in policy was ever present (Millett, 1952, pp. 472–478).

The Educational Policies Commission-ACE report (1951, p. 44) summarized the situation: "It may be said that an armed force 'in being' of 3,500,000 will, within a relatively short time, require at least two years of service of every able-bodied young man. The precise timing of that service is less significant in the arithmetic of manpower than its inclusion in the total flow. While all are needed, sufficient flexibility exists in the possible sources available to permit some adjustment in the timing of service where this appears to be in the national interest."

Much discussion dealt with the proper timing—the advantages and disadvantages of college training before military service, the fairness of educational deferments, the immediacy of need for certain specialized manpower, the relative long-term national need for civilian welfare specializations, inequities arising from local selective service administration, ways and means of maintaining enrolment flow, and the meaning of military service for equality of educational opportunity. Everyone understood that enrolments scarcely could be projected for more than a year at a time and that stability in tenure, educational innovation, and all income-related activity would be seriously affected.

The debate on universal military training had an effect beyond concern with enrolments and size of student bodies. Bolman (1951, p. 229) referred to "the extent the international situation has shaken the foundations of higher education in the United States." Whether men who had served in the armed forces for two years would continue their education worried both parents and educators. The impact of two years lost on the intellectual and professional life of the nation was a still larger question. "Educators throughout the country had been thinking in terms of ever-expanding opportunity for those who previously would not have gone to college. Now the reforms needed for the anticipated enlarged constituency would be cut short by national military service and training" (Bolman, 1951, p. 229).

The uncertainty about enrolment tied directly to uncertainty about finance. Tuition and fee income is an important source of funding current and planned expenditures. In 1950, private universities received 65.3 percent of educational income from student charges; independent liberal arts colleges, 72.9 percent; and private professional schools 59.7 percent. By the same measure of student charges, public universities in 1950 received 30.9 percent of educational income from this source; liberal arts colleges, 24.7 percent; and professional schools, 30.6 percent (Millett, 1952, pp. 300–01).

Such figures help us to understand the depressed Cold War mood of the early fifties. In 1949–50 enrolments increased by 5 percent and institutional operating expenditures increased by 12.11 percent from their 1947–48 levels. In 1951–52 both enrolments and expenditures were down—enrolments by 13.8

percent and expenditures by 5.03 percent (dollars deflated to 1957).[1]

The unease in the financial situation was accentuated by growing inflation. The Educational Policies Commission (1951, p. 2) called inflation "the most urgent economic problem" in the immediate future." When deflated to 1930 price levels, per student educational expenditures decreased from $289 in 1930 to $277 in 1950. The same index stood at $291 in 1940 (Millett, 1952, p. 116). What had seemed to be moderate improvement was an actual decline when inflation was considered—and 1930 was not necessarily a sound base. By estimating what normal maintenance of quality required, the institutions should have spent some 17 percent more than was available. "By some such amount higher education failed to reach its desirable potentialities in 1950" (Millett, 1952, p. 118).

Henry T. Heald, chancellor of New York University in 1951, analyzed the administrative dilemmas of the times: "Fluctuations in enrolment, inflation and the rising cost of living, and better-paying opportunities in business and industry haunt educational administrators who try to assemble and maintain capable teaching and research personnel. Many persons who have entered academic life through choice, to do the thing they like to do, are hard put to maintain an adequate standard of living for themselves and their families. . . . Shifting enrolment makes some positions unstable and advancement uncertain" (American Council on Education, 1952, p. 19).

The faculty salary situation, and its threat to morale, had been anticipated by the President's Commission on Higher Education in 1947. Surveys for the commission indicated that faculty members were greatly disturbed. "Fifty percent felt that present incomes were such that continuance in the teaching profession was at a great personal sacrifice; that the quality of their work was being seriously affected by financial worries. It seems evident that the favorable report upon faculty morale will soon be succeeded by an unfavorable one unless faculty salaries are made

[1]Deflated income figures from O'Neil (1971, p. 92). Enrolment figures from U.S. Office of Education (1956, p. 2).

more adequate (President's Commission on Higher Education, 1947, *4*, p. 50).

Salary studies for the commission revealed that after 14 years of experience, physicians had an average net income twice as high as that of the college teacher. The average real estate salesman would have 50 percent more net income. From 1940–1947, the cost of living had increased about 57 percent while faculty salaries were raised 32 percent. "The professor in 1947 taught more students, worked longer hours, shouldered graver responsibilities, and received substantially less real income than he did in 1940." The situation could be changed only by "sharply increased public and private support of higher education (President's Commission on Higher Education, 1947, *4*, p. 52).

With unchecked inflation, uncertain student fee income, uncertain appropriations, an uncertain climate for philanthropy, and demands for increasing service, what did the future hold for funding operations?

The prospect for increased support was not reassuring. Long (1951, pp. 410–411), a faculty member at Greenville College, Illinois, surveyed 40 small colleges with five hundred to seven hundred students to determine if administrators were planning for what he saw as "the crisis ahead." Evidently they were, as shown by the resulting list of steps these institutions were taking in the two broad areas of supplementing current income and methods for retrenchment of expenditures. Long concluded, "Contrary to the wish of every forward looking college president this period seems to be one of precaution, of hedging, and of retrenchment" (Long, 1951, pp. 410–411).

Proposals for economy, many uninformed and unworkable, are characteristic in such a dilemma, not unlike the plight of higher education in the thirties and in the seventies. Undoubtedly, in such a large enterprise some economics could be and were found. Attacks on proliferation of courses, excessive specialization, large libraries, unchanged instructional practices, limited institutional cooperation, class size, and business operations were common and sometimes justified. Some responses such as regional interinstitutional cooperation were more constructive than budget cutting. These responses were reflected in the development of the Southern Regional Educational Board, the Western Interstate Commission on Higher Education, and the New England Board on Higher Education. Their impact was not general, however, nor central in institutional life, and their programs grew slowly. Innovations and economies alone, then as now, could not offer a final solution without impairing the contribution of higher education to the national well-being and without limiting the quantity and quality of educational opportunity. The Commission on Financing Higher Education (1952, pp. 109–110) observed: "The pressure to economize is not new to colleges and universities. They have felt it for years and have constantly attempted to stretch their funds as far as possible. It is curious that about this enterprise that generally lives on the verge of genteel poverty there has grown up a myth of wasteful and conspicuous spending. . . . Where efficiency can so easily be made an excuse for economies that undermine the educational service, the real danger is financial stringency, not extravagance."

The search for operational funds could not ignore the shortage of physical plants. From 1918 and perhaps earlier to 1950, campuses had not been able to match physical plant and equipment with enrolment growth and the increasing demand for varied service, including research. Wars, depression, and inflation had left huge deficits by any measure of adequacy. At no time did resources meet accumulated and new post-crisis needs. Further, as knowledge grew more complex, particularly in the sciences, costs increased beyond those of historic growth. The staff of the Commission on Financing Higher Education estimated that nearly $3.5 billion for new instructional plant facilities and $720 million for new residential plants was needed for the 1950–1960 decade (Millett, 1952, p. 263).

In the twentieth century world of knowledge, quality of instruction and of research are dependent upon the tools of learning. Equipment, space, and libraries are the means to effective teaching and research. An adequate physical plant is central to quality performance. How to fund a minimal plant at a time of fiscal uncertainty varies with the individual case—by gifts, loans, fees, or government appropriations. In the fifties, no one answer could solve the general problem—and the deficit was to become a legacy for the sixties. To survive, each institution had to find its own resources, if any.

Another result of the wartime atmosphere discouraged the profession and the institutions as well. Education faced the necessity of supporting the national goal of military preparedness and at the same time maintaining freedom of thought and expression in teaching and in the search for new knowledge. The Educational Policies Commission and the American Council on Education in 1951 jointly sponsored a conference on "Education and National Security." Arthur Adams, then president of the American Council on Education, posed the problem: "The adjustment to the military manpower needs on the one hand and to the strengthening of the spirit and ideals of democracy on the other can be, and sometimes is, interpreted by different segments of the public as evidence that educators have become warmongers or that they are pacifists or that they are Communist sympathizers. To steer a straight course . . . is not an easy task. Yet it is the task of educators to concern themselves with all of the manifold activities in which the potent force of free education can contribute to make ours a society in which material strength is not sought as an end in itself but only as an instrument to insure the freedom of the mind and the cultivation of the spirit of each individual" (American Council on Education, 1952, p. vii). The political confusion was identified: "America faces the problem of treason in a degree and manner unknown to our past experience and shocking to the assumptions by which we live. Conversely, the effort to make political capital of the fear and the fact of treason has led to reckless character assassination and inflamed public thinking (Educational Policies Commission and others, 1951, p. 2).

Thus, we are introduced to the era of Senator Joseph McCarthy.

For most people in the academic community and for many other thoughtful people, the term "McCarthyism" has come to mean the exploitation of a complex public issue for political gain by means of unproved allegations, name calling and innuendo, character assassination, institutional slander, guilt by association, and manipulation of publicity to smother opposition. Initially, the avowed issue was the extent of communist involvement in the affairs of the nation; later, the issue became the threat posed to the integrity of the legislative process by McCarthy's unscrupulous, demagogic drive for political power.

For some, of course, McCarthyism meant something quite different. They equated the term with "Americanism" or patriotism in a fight against a declared enemy. Still others were only concerned about the issue of "communism in government" and accepted the misrepresentations, exaggerations and unsubstantiated accusations as a necessary evil in getting to the core of the concern. As an example, the White House almost rejected a nominee for the directorship of the Atomic Energy Commission because the nominee's wife had twice been to tea at the Russian Embassy. The objection was not sustained, but the White House spokesman feared "the atmosphere on the Hill" (Conant, 1970, p. 562). A relevant question remains unanswered, however, although many explanations have been offered: Why were the normal legal, constitutional, cultural, and procedural restraints virtually paralyzed in the presence of a ruthless attack on the civil liberties of individuals and on the exercise of public duty by honorable men (Griffith, 1970, p. 116)?

It is possible now to reflect upon McCarthyism as a result of the concatenation of circumstances that exploded in the fifties, not as the creation of one man or as an aberration of mid-century politics. "What came to be called 'McCarthyism' was grounded in a set of attitudes, assumptions, and judgments with deep roots in American history." The fear of radicalism has had expression in many incidents, from the Alien and Sedition Acts in the early years of the United States government to the Sacco and Vanzetti case in the early twenties. The Bolshevik Revolution was the source of apprehension, and Soviet Communism "has informed and in some instances dominated American politics for more than fifty years." The Dies Committee, formed in 1938, "pioneered the whole spectrum of slogans, techniques, and political mythologies that would later be called 'McCarthyism.' " In the years immediately following the war,

Congress projected some 35 "investigating" committees and many of them, whatever their charge, tried to latch on to the increasingly popular "communists in government" issue (Griffith, 1970, pp. 30–32).

It is not the purpose here to analyze the political turmoil of the fifties, the history of McCarthyism, or the outcome of the political conflict it engendered. However, higher education was caught in the crossfire and the unanswered question as to how institutions and academic people would come out of the situation and what would be the effect on the stability of higher education was an acknowledged uncertainty of the times.

It was not the Washington scene alone that threatened colleges and universities. The investigating committees of the Congress could undertake only a limited number of subjects, call a limited number of witnesses, and issue a limited number of reports. "Loyalty" investigations of federal employees did not include many members of the academic community.[2] The acquiescence of the executive departments to Congressional pressures on appointments and discharges, the book-banning in U.S. Information Centers abroad, and the results of other fulminations of McCarthy and his political allies did not often directly reach into the operations of colleges and universities. It was the fear that these political powers might strike the local campus that created uncertainty about the manner of organized resistance to the obvious violation of civil liberties and the accepted code of fair procedure. What was more important, the national scenario was imitated at state and community levels. "Little McCarthy committees" in state legislatures became common, their procedures based upon the pattern of star-chamber and inquisition, often with anonymous informers. Textbook materials were assailed on a priori judgments. Unsubstantiated accusations against people, institutions, and publications were given serious attention. Local newspapers ran stories based on

[2] However, the program affected some 10 million workers during the Eisenhower administration: 2.5 million federal employees, 3.5 million in the armed forces, 3 million in private industry, half a million merchant seamen and port workers, and 100,000 of the Atomic Energy Commission (Cook, 1971, p. 558).

unproved suspicions that tended to erode confidence in the institutions; the incidents were many. In short, the McCarthy allies created confusion across the land and responsible citizens did not know how to deal with unrestrained irrationality. At the national level, these allies included senators and representatives who had preceded McCarthy in exploiting the "communism in government" issue, a "large group of right-wing newspapermen" (and radio commentators) and financial "angels" who supported such magazines as "Plain Talk," "The Freeman," and "Counterattack" (Griffith, 1970, pp. 62–64).

The House Un-American Activities Committee early indicated that colleges and universities were objects of investigation. In 1949, the committee asked for lists of textbooks and of supplemental reading from more than one hundred colleges and universities, and also sought to have the FBI make loyalty investigations of "potential" recipients of NSF and AEC fellowships. The committee proposed screening of foreign citizens invited to visit the United States under leadership, education, or orientation programs. Institutional and editorial protests stopped the implementation of these plans, but the developing strategy was revealed (Brown, 1950, pp. 8–9). Senator McCarthy himself defined it (quoted in De Mello, 1968, pp. 54–55):

> The average American can do very little insofar as digging Communists, espionage agents, out of our government is concerned. They must depend upon those of us whom they send down here to man the watchtowers of the nation. The thing that the American people can do is to be vigilant day and night to make sure they don't have Communists teaching the sons and daughters of America. Now, I realize that the minute anyone tries to get a Communist out of a college, out of a university, there'll be raised the phony cry that you're interfering with academic freedom. I would like to emphasize that there is no academic freedom where a Communist is concerned. He is not a free agent. He has no freedom of thought, no freedom of expression. He must take his orders from

Moscow, or he will no longer be a member of the
Communist Party. I may say . . . I don't care how
much of a screwball or a crackpot any professor or
teacher may be as long as he or she is a free agent.
But once, once you have this United States, from the
Atlantic to the Pacific, covered with a network of
professors and teachers who are getting their orders
from Moscow, from an organization that wants to de-
stroy this nation, that wants to corrupt the minds of
youth, then . . . we're rapidly losing the battle.

After much soul-searching, consensus developed within
the academic community, as elsewhere, that the Communist
Party was a conspiracy rather than a political party as ordinarily
understood, and that no card-carrying member of the party
should be employed by a college or university.[3] Some difficult
questions then arose. What about former members of the party
who had renounced their association? Should a teacher who took
the Fifth Amendment on the question of party membership be
excluded from appointment or made subject to dismissal? What
criteria should be used in determining a communist front and
how should membership in a front organization be regarded in
relation to academic employment or student privileges?[4] How
could a teacher whose subject included the study of Communism be protected against the criticism that he was "teaching
Communism"? Should an institution initiate a properly safe-
guarded inquiry of its own when a faculty member was accused
or wait for the FBI or another agency to deal with the matter
first? What procedure should be followed in considering visiting campus speakers who were admitted Communists? Should a
student group with alleged Communist affiliations be given
campus standing? Should state-administered "loyalty oaths" be

---

[3] See statements by the Association of American Universities, 1953, 1962.
Also, see Educational Policies Commission, 1949.
[4] The AAU statement said, "If an instructor follows Communist practice
by becoming a propagandist for one opinion, adopting a 'party line,'
silencing criticism or impairing freedom of thought and expression in his
classroom he forfeits not only all university support but his right to membership in the university" (1962, Section 4, n.p.).

resisted institutionally? (California, Massachusetts, and Illinois were among the states adopting loyalty oaths for teachers, an issue that persisted into the sixties.) There was no consensus on these questions, and the response to each incident had to be hammered out in an atmosphere where "treason" was a word easily employed.

New court decisions, new legislation, and new public attitudes make it difficult to understand in retrospect the impact of the demagoguery that restrained even the president from speaking out against it as forcefully as he felt, to overlook the duress under which academic leaders operated, and to appreciate fully the doubt in the public mind as to the capability of their educational institutions to cope with the alleged communist infiltration.

Although the number of people convicted of spying or otherwise aiding the acknowledged enemy was not large, the cases were of a kind that undermined confidence. Also, the number of those who took the Fifth Amendment in the judicial process was disconcerting, even though they were not brought to trial or formal judgment. Some faculty members were among them. The position of these educators could be justified in terms of opposing thought control and intrusion upon private beliefs. On the other hand, lack of candor about public business, such as teaching, did not fit well into the academic tradition. Each case had to be examined on its own merits, and publicity about each case—headlines, editorials, petitions, protests, hearings, and investigations—added to the public inflammation.

From the most comprehensive collection of faculty experiences recorded soon after the height of the McCarthy era (the spring of 1955), a picture emerges of the ways in which normal faculty activities were disrupted. Lazarsfeld and Thielens (1958, pp. 192–236) provide their observations of social science faculty, revealing evidence of caution among colleagues, constraints in the classroom, impaired relationships with students, constraints on professional work outside the classroom, on nonprofessional activities of teachers, and the endangered self-respect of the professor. While careful to point out that the majority of faculty members they interviewed "felt no curtailment of their own academic freedom or that of colleagues," Lazarsfeld and Thielens (1958, p. 196) go on to discuss in detail their belief that their findings "suggest consistently that a noticeable segment of our respondents and their colleagues felt intimidated by the difficult years—deterred by fear of attack and of harm to their careers that might result from a free expression of their views."

The student mood was one of withdrawal and acquiescence. Politics was characterized as "dirty business." Those who objected strenuously to the excesses risked considerable personal damage. Conforming or remaining silent seemed to be the best way out. In one history class, "a majority of the students voted in favor of Socrates' execution. It made quite a stir among the professors, but the students showed little surprise . . . or concern" (Cook, 1971, pp. 19–20). Other factors were a part of the explanation for "the silent generation," but the political atmosphere was undoubtedly an important influence.

In 1953, the President of the American Council on Education acknowledged, "There is no doubt about the reality of the public unrest about education. It is here and now. . . . There are many people who are honestly discouraged, who are fearful, who are uninformed, but sincerely concerned" (Adams, 1953, p. 15). Once again, as in previous times of stress, the educational community became aware tardily of the need for public understanding. "The educator, the administrator, may not remain today in an ivory tower. It is his job, really, to get into the community . . . to make the community aware of the true meaning of education" (Sachar, 1953, p. 27).

Certainly the ebullience of colleges and universities during the early postwar period was modified by the realities of the fifties. The uncertainty, resulting largely from the troubled state of the nation, would later be resolved by external forces and conditions. But "what priority for higher education?" was the emerging rhetorical question of the times (Henry, 1961).

# 7

# Increasing Enrolment and the Struggle for Resources

Before the end of the fifties, a new concern was apparent. The educational ferment subsided and the uncertainties faded in the preoccupation of universities with enrolment projections, which were receiving wide public attention as early as 1956. (As a description of what lay ahead, the term *tidal wave,* which came to have wide usage, was unfortunate. The connotation of disaster was hardly appropriate.)

It is difficult to understand the slow comprehension and acceptance of projected enrolment increases, despite public information. Thoughtful analysts of population data published the national implications as early as 1953 (Thompson, 1954, p. 215). Regional studies had been made earlier. However, these commentaries did not remove the prevailing concern with the enrolment dip between 1950 and 1954 and the uncertainty created by such factors as recession, military demand for manpower, and inability to forecast new factors that would influence the rate of increase. By 1955, new numbers had been counted and partially charted. That there would be increased levels was beyond debate, although the precise increase could not be anticipated. But public discussion was minimal and public interest and concern did not jell until after the Second Report of the President's Committee on Education Beyond the High School (1957). The National Defense Education Act providing for student aid and specialized training was enacted in 1958, and the Higher Education Facilities Act was passed in 1963. Hence, over a decade elapsed before a realistic federal response was made to evident social needs.

The First Interim Report of the President's Committee on Education Beyond the High School, published in November 1956, predicted that enrolment in colleges and universities would double or perhaps triple by 1970.

The report further predicted that other millions would be seeking nondegree education and training in private technical and occupational training schools, as well as by correspondence, educational television, apprentice training, adult education, and other programs. "We are achieving in this country mass wealth, mass goods, mass leisure, and mass opportunities for further education. . . . These undisputed facts present the American people and their educational system with their greatest challenge and their greatest opportunity" (President's Committee on Education Beyond the High School, 1956, p. 2).

The projections proved to be near to the mark, as Table 4 reveals.

The increasing percentage of high school students who were graduated and the increasing percentage of these high school graduates who enroled in post-high school education were principal factors in the unanticipated enrolment growth. This was observed before the effects of the post-1940 so-called "baby boom" began to be felt at the college level (Thompson, 1956, p. 93).

Opinions vary as to the reasons for this development. Business and industry were placing a higher premium on advanced education. The personnel demands created by large organization and increasing technology were met by curriculum developments within the institutions, and increasing numbers of students enroled in college to prepare for new careers as well as for the traditional ones. Furthermore, credentialism increased

Table 4. Opening fall enrolments, all institutions of higher education

| | *Degree credit enrolment*[a] | *Percentage increase each half-decade* |
|------|------|------|
| 1955 | 2,678,623 | |
| 1960 | 3,610,007 | 35 |
| 1965 | 5,570,271 | 108 |
| 1970 | 7,920,149 | 196 |

[a] The degree credit category includes students enroled in resident and extension courses whose work is creditable toward the award of an academic degree.

Summary tables on noncollege post-high school education for the same period are not available, but separate indices indicate that growth in these areas was comparable.

*Source:* American Council on Education. *A Fact Book on Higher Education* (Issue No. 1, Enrollment Data), 1974, p. 748.

in the general job market and degrees became more important. Handlin and Handlin (1970, p. 72) observe: "Bureaucratic organizations required credentials of those they hired: unions set tight requirements around valuable positions; and mechanization eased the need for hands. The high school graduate, unwanted on the labor market, had a desperate need for the college degree; and the number of families that could afford to assist their children to that goal rose with the general increase of incomes."

The influence of the veterans was often overlooked in assessing the new popularity of college. Among the millions who enroled with G.I. benefits were many who otherwise would not have gone to college. As these veterans returned to home and job, generally satisfied with their experience in higher education, their example was obvious to the younger generation and an influence on public opinion as to the values of higher education.

Public opinion increasingly centered on social and civic values as well as career economics. The university as the home of science and research, for example, was held in higher respect. The philosophical position of the President's Commission report of 1947 seems to have had more acceptance as the years passed. It conceived of the college as a service to society and spoke of the need for scholars with "a passionate concern for human betterment, for the improvement of social conditions, and of relations among men." Such educators would "apply at the point of social action what the social scientist had discovered regarding the laws of human behavior." The colleges were to become "laboratories of inter-race and interfaith fellowship" by eliminating all forms of discrimination. For every student, colleges would offset "the handicaps of secondary school instruction which is of poor quality," and they would undertake massive programs of adult education (President's Commission on Higher Education, 1947, 2, pp. 26, 42).

Another important element in the projected enrolment increase lay in demographic factors. Not only had the birthrate increased between 1940 and 1955, but there was lower infant mortality. The increase in persons of college age would be greater than the past increase in relation to the number of births (Brown, 1955, pp. 1–6).

The general background for an era of growth was described by the President's Committee on Education Beyond the High School (1957, pp. 16–17): "Revolutionary changes are occurring in American education of which even yet we are only dimly aware. This Nation has been propelled into a challenging new educational era since World War II by the convergence of powerful forces—an explosion of knowledge and population, a burst of technological and economic advance, the outbreak of ideological conflict and the uprooting of old political and cultural patterns on a worldwide scale, and an unparalleled demand by Americans for more and better education. . . . These forces have created enormously increased educational challenges of which we have not taken full stock and which our educational institutions as a whole are ill-prepared to meet. The gap between this Nation's educational needs and its educational effort is widening ominously."

Although opinion was not unanimous, the prevailing view held that there no longer need be much concern about educating too many people. It was predicted that a 75 percent increase in professional and technical personnel would be needed by 1975 (President's Commission on Education Beyond the High School, 1957, p. 1). Peter Drucker, noted business analyst, indicated that automation would bring a demand for "incredibly large numbers of men . . . in new highly skilled jobs" and that large numbers of highly educated people would be needed in "new jobs as designers of machinery, draftsmen, system engineers, mathematicians or logicians." Also, increased numbers would be needed for "new managerial jobs requiring a high ability to think, to analyze, to make decisions, and to assume risks" (Drucker, 1955, p. 44). Also see Trytten (1955, pp. 17–21).

### Enlarging Capacity

Although the conferences and committee reports repeatedly emphasized that the period ahead would provide a new opportunity for higher education, the institutions grimly took stock of the requirements for new space, new equipment, and additional personnel. Already underfinanced since 1930, administrators responsible for operations anticipated an unprecedented scramble for resources. The President's Committee on Education (1957) built its recommendations around the need for teachers, the need for assistance to students, the need for expansion and diversity of educational opportunities, and the need for funds, with emphasis upon the federal role. Some educators, of course, advocated greater selectivity in admissions as a means of restricting growth, but they were minor voices even in the private sector (American Council on Education, 1955, p. 2).

The first need obviously would be for space. By 1956 there had not been much gain in reducing the capital deficit which had been estimated at over $4 billion; see Chapter Six. "When children born in the last sixteen years come to college, they will create a problem that cannot be solved by temporary overcrowding such as was done to accommodate the GIs in the 1940s" (Perkins, 1955, p. 102). Nonetheless, some expediencies would have to be adopted. It would take years to meet specific needs in a given institution with plans, financial underwriting, contracts, and construction. Improved space utilization, redirection of students to institutions with space, and continued use of temporary facilities would be taken for granted. Compacts for interinstitutional use of facilities would be encouraged. Local and state resources, particularly for community colleges and public universities, would be increased. Even without an accurate inventory of facilities or consensus on the most efficient use of space, some federal action would be required to prevent a massive denial of educational opportunity and a diminution of instructional quality. In 1956, the capital needs for a decade were estimated to be $13 billion—thought to be a conservative figure (Dobbins, 1956, p. 102).

A program of matching federal grants for instructional facilities was enacted in 1963 and the first appropriations were made in 1965. The program was based on precedents inherent in the Public Works Administration of the thirties, the Surplus Property Act of 1944, the College Housing Loan provisions of the Housing Act of 1950, the program for matching grants for research facilities in medicine, dentistry, and public health, and the very successful Hill-Burton Act for expansion of hospitals. This action was a major development in federal assistance to higher education; both private and public institutions were eligible. The program provided significant general institutional aid by releasing resources to be used for high priority needs other than buildings; it could be adjusted or terminated in terms of need without a commitment as to a continuing federal policy for institutional assistance.

The plan was a central recommendation of the President's Committee on Education Beyond the High School (1957, p. 89, 100) and was widely endorsed by higher education institutions and organizations. The extent of awards made is shown here (figures for 1964–67 from U.S. Department of Health, Education and Welfare, 1967, pp. 60–63; for 1968–69, from U.S. Department of Health, Education and Welfare, 1969, 1970 supplement, pp. 2, 14, 6):

| 1964 | None |
|------|------|
| 1965 | 286,131,306 |
| 1966 | 528,794,000 |
| 1967 | 517,720,000 |
| 1968 | 282,000,000 |
| 1969 | 223,920,000 |
| | 1,838,565,306 |

The question of where to get teachers was another wide-spread concern in the late fifties. The question applied first to the teachers needed at once in the elementary schools; others were needed in the high schools and in college preparatory curricula, and soon more would be needed in the colleges generally. "With industry, production, the armed forces, education and other agencies competing for trained youth, the teaching profession will be sorely tried to meet the needs," predicted Thompson (1954, p. 4), one of the earlier analysts and interpreters of the Tidal Wave. Two hundred fifty thousand elementary and secondary teachers would be needed within the next six years, and additional thousands in the succeeding period. Even the expediencies hardly desirable—of requesting teachers to remain on duty until age 70, resorting to temporary certification, and altering requirements for certification—would have little impact on solving the over-all problem.

Estimates of the need for additional college teachers in the sixties varied greatly, from 50,000 to 250,000, depending upon the estimates of enrolment increases and rate increases. The aggregate college staff in 1952–53 was approximately 200,000. While some building planning was underway, new scholarship programs announced, new programs projected, no general plan for supplying the teachers had been seriously considered in 1955. Each institution seemed confident that it could raid another or that some solution would turn up.

The President's Committee on Education (1957, pp. 27, 29) gave focus to the subject both in quantitative and qualitative terms. The committee pointed out the unfavorable economic position of the profession in relationship to other careers and the danger of "cumulative deterioration of the educational process" as recruitment for the talented became more competitive. In addition to salary improvement, the committee recognized the need for organized recruitment, retention of older teachers, expansion and strengthening of graduate programs, and "finding ways to teach larger numbers without loss of quality."

But above all, improvement of faculty salaries would be at the center of recruitment effectiveness. Teaching, the committee said, "is the only major occupation in which there has been a relative and, in the senior ranks, an absolute deterioration of economic status in this century. It is probably the only profession which has failed to share significantly in the general prosperity of the past decade or more. . . . Quite frequently the starting salary of the young graduate entering business or industry is higher than the pay of the experienced teacher who has just prepared him. . . . To induce or accept much larger numbers of students into a system of higher education which cannot provide adequate resources of competent teachers would be a national fraud and calamity (President's Committee on Education Beyond the High School, 1957, p. 35). The combination of modest increases in salaries throughout the decade of the 1940s and heavy inflation following World War II seriously eroded the purchasing power of faculty incomes. Baumol and Heim (1965, pp. 248–49) estimate that for all faculty ranks combined "purchasing power in 1964 dollars fell from about $8,500 in 1939 to less than $7,000 one decade later."

The key recommendation of the committee was that the average faculty income level be doubled within five or ten years, and that other fringe benefits and inducements be added liberally. The recommendation became a reality, as the following table will show. The shortage of staff intensified the competition, of course. The change was given an enormous boost by the favorable public evaluation of higher education that prevailed roughly from 1958 to 1968, including the public reaction to the challenge of Sputnik, discussed in the following chapter. The prewar salary level for all ranks combined was recovered and exceeded by 1958–59. For the next ten years, the purchasing power of faculty salaries increased regularly, as the figures in Table 5 show.

At a time when higher education was challenged to gear up for phenomenal increases in enrolment, it is interesting that considerable attention would be given to improved student counseling and increased financial assistance to students. With more students than capacity in prospect, why were these subjects of concern?

Counseling was perceived as an aid to wise student choices for whatever locations were available. Furthermore, the new student body would not only be larger but more diverse in background, motivation, and ability. Those aspiring to occupa-

Table 5. Growth rates of faculty compensation all ranks combined
1955–1969

| Years | Percentage total increase | Percentage inflationary offset | Percentage increase in real purchasing power |
|---|---|---|---|
| 1955–57[a] | 6.9 | 2.5 | 4.4 |
| 1957–59 | 5.7 | 1.8 | 3.9 |
| 1960–61[b] | 6.5 | 1.5 | 5.0 |
| 1961–62 | 5.8 | 1.0 | 4.8 |
| 1962–63 | 5.0 | 1.7 | 3.3 |
| 1963–64 | 6.0 | 1.6 | 4.4 |
| 1964–65 | 7.3 | 1.4 | 5.9 |
| 1965–66 | 6.8 | 3.2 | 3.6 |
| 1966–67 | 7.4 | 2.8 | 4.6 |
| 1967–68 | 7.2 | 4.2 | 3.0 |
| 1968–69 | 7.1 | 5.4 | 1.7 |

[a] Data for 1955–59 taken from Committee Z on the Economic Status of the Profession, *55*, June 1969, p. 193.
[b] Data for 1960–69 taken from Committee Z on the Economic Status of the Profession, *56*, June 1970, p. 176.

tions requiring less than degree preparation might find community colleges more suitable. Other kinds of post-high school education might help lighten the load on colleges and universities. That half the academically superior students in terms of high school grades were not going to college received concerned attention; the social demand for trained brainpower could not afford such waste of talent. Similarly, the loss of exceptional students among the economically underprivileged was noted, as was the under-representation of blacks and other racial and ethnic groups. These premises had all been set forth, with documentation, by the Education for Democracy report of 1947 (President's Commission on Higher Education) and were noted again, reinforced and updated, by the President's Committee on Education Beyond the High School in 1957.

### Scramble for Resources

*Higher Education: Who Pays? Who Benefits? Who Should Pay?* is the title of a report by the Carnegie Commission on Higher Education, June 1973. The questions asked are old ones and over the years have had varied arguments and different answers. Some contend that the individual, because he personally benefits, should pay the full cost of his instruction, although there is no agreement on how to compute full cost. Others claim that higher education should be fully subsidized, as are elementary and secondary education, because of its social benefits and necessity in a democratic society. The practice has been to charge what the institutions thought the market would bear and (within institutional objectives) could be justified by institutional needs.

This practice of expediency has applied both to the public and private sectors. Public institutions were established originally as free education, but compromise with reality has brought them to high charges—"high" when one considers the original intent. Most public community colleges are still tuition-free or have relatively low charges. Private institutions originally intended modest fees, to be set at a level that would not establish economic barriers to admission. Fiscal difficulties, however, have brought student charges in the private sector to a point where there is serious concern that their students may be predominantly from upper income families and that a significant number of private institutions may be "priced out of the market."

In 1955–1965, the key question was whether student charges could be increased to sustain the proportion of institutional support that they had come to represent. Basic costs would rise to meet both inflation and the increased costs of extended services and facilities required for larger enrolments. The question can now be answered in the affirmative, as Table 6 reveals.

That the proportion of educational income derived from student charges actually increased slightly, in both public and private sectors, is truly remarkable when one considers the dollar levels to which they have risen. The increase in student financial aid—from gifts, institutional revenues, and state and federal programs—significantly contributed to this result, as did loan funds and work-study opportunities. The availability of urban universities and community colleges to commuting

Table 6. Aggregate tuition revenues as a proportion of total
educational funds for higher education
Selected Years 1951–1969

| Year | Public institutions | | Private institutions | | All institutions | |
|---|---|---|---|---|---|---|
| | *Tuition income* | *Total educational funds* | *Tuition income* | *Total educational funds* | *Tuition income* | *Total educational funds* |
| 1951–52 | $ 116.2 (12.2%) | $ 953.1 | $ 330.4 (45.6%) | $ 724.9 | $ 446.6 (26.6%) | $ 1,678.0 |
| 1955–56 | 203.0 (14.7%) | 1,381.9 | 522.9 (55.0%) | 950.4 | 725.9 (31.0%) | 2,342.3 |
| 1961–62 | 429.7 (15.7%) | 2,735.5 | 1,075.6 (56.0%) | 1,919.4 | 1,505.3 (32.3%) | 4,654.9 |
| 1965–66 | 864.0 (17.2%) | 5,015.6 | 1,835.7 (58.3%) | 3,147.5 | 2,699.7 (33.1%) | 8,163.1 |
| 1969–70 | 1,640 (16.5%) | 9,932.5 | 2,690.0 (58.9%) | 4,565.0 | 4,330.0 (29.9%) | 14,497.5 |

Dollar figures in millions.
*Source:* Carnegie Commission on Higher Education. *Higher Education: Who Benefits? Who Pays? Who Should Pay?* New York: McGraw-Hill, 1973.

students is not reflected in these student aid figures. Without the expanded capacity of these institutions, the account of containing the Tidal Wave would have been significantly different. Although enrolment figures for urban institutions collectively are not readily available, those which are available for community and junior colleges offer an index to this expanded capacity—see Table 7.

Questions were asked in 1955 that are still being asked today. To what extent can tuition rates be expected to rise further? Is student aid currently at a level that lessens equal educational opportunity? Is the public subsidy of student aid fair to the noncollege student and should he be granted a comparable public benefit? Where is the justified dividing line, socially and educationally, between universal access and universal attendance?

Even though these questions could not be answered, the scramble of resources went on. And in that scramble, the Tidal Wave reached an evolutionary climax of federal involvement

**Table 7. Growth in number of two-year institutions
and their degree credit enrolments 1955–1970**

| Fall of | Number of institutions | Total degree credit enrolment | Percentage increase in enrolment |
|---|---|---|---|
| 1955 | 467 | 308,411 | |
| 1960 | 521 | 451,333 | 46 |
| 1965 | 633 | 841,437 | 173 |
| 1970 | 827 | 1,629,982 | 430 |

*Note:* Degree credit enrolment category includes students enroled in resident or extension courses whose work is creditable towards the awarding of an academic degree. Enrolments in nondegree courses reflect a similar pattern of increase.
*Source:* National Center for Educational Statistics, 1974, p. 83.

in the support of higher education. Meanwhile, student assistance grew to massive proportions—see Table 8.

Related to the drive for student assistance was concern that students be able to meet the inevitable increase in charges that would have to be imposed to meet the rising costs of inflation, expansion of facilities, and new programs for a larger student population. Undoubtedly student charges necessarily would continue to be a principal source of educational income for private institutions and an important one for public institutions. Maintenance of at least the current proportion of educational expenditures supported by student charges was one of the incentives for enlarged programs of student assistance and for their priority among institutional efforts.

It must also be remembered that the public interest in science and in an enlarged national capability in science—generated by Sputnik (see Chapter Eight)—was a major factor in the rapid increase of federal assistance to students, graduate and undergraduate.

As the implications of the data on the rising tide of students eligible for higher education came to fuller understanding, first on the part of the academic community, then by other sectors and the general public, the issues all seemed

Table 8. Estimated student aid expenditures (in millions of dollars)

| | Veterans benefits | Social Security dependents benefits | State scholarship programs | Public sources | Institutional expenditure from Private sources | Current funds | Direct private aid | Total |
|---|---|---|---|---|---|---|---|---|
| 1955–56 | $ 432.1 | | $ 5.0 | $ 14.0 | $ 39.0 | $ 43.2 | $14.5 | $ 547.8 |
| 1957–58 | 421.4 | | 10.0 | 20.1 | 51.4 | 59.8 | 18.8 | 581.5 |
| 1959–60 | 233.1 | | 15.0 | 26.4 | 67.9 | 79.8 | 23.2 | 445.4 |
| 1961–62 | 82.9 | | 27.0 | 34.4 | 85.9 | 111.0 | 27.1 | 368.3 |
| 1963–64 | 25.1 | | 44.0 | 50.1 | 100.7 | 152.6 | 30.4 | 402.9 |
| 1965–66 | | $207.0 | 72.0 | 120.5 | 141.8 | 166.9 | 37.8 | 746.0 |
| 1967–68 | 334.9 | 305.0 | 120.0 | 330.0 | 173.9 | 214.8 | 40.7 | 1,519.3 |
| 1969–70 | 665.1 | 401.0 | 200.0 | 470.0 | 230.0 | 300.0 | 43.3 | 2,309.4 |
| 1970–71 | 1,117.3 | 455.0 | 236.0 | 575.0 | 273.0 | 380.0 | 48.0 | 3,084.3 |

Note: Amounts do not include loan funds provided to students since they represent revolving funds. Interest on loans which is forgiven while students are in school is included.
Source: Carnegie Commission on Higher Education. Higher Education: Who Benefits? Who Pays? Who Should Pay? New York: McGraw-Hill, 1973.

to be related mainly to finance and to ways and means of providing the necessary services. Possible economies, new methods and technologies for instruction, and new structures of organization were proposed. The necessities for interinstitutional and statewide planning, both voluntary and mandatory, were reviewed and sometimes implemented; institutional goals were reassessed. Evaluation of these and other approaches to preparing for the new load was continuous, but all these efforts combined could not relieve the necessity for an enormous amount of new funding. Moreover, the increasing costs of inflation compounded the difficulty, although not in the proportions later seen in the seventies.

An alternative to increased funding, of course, was to restrict educational opportunity. The question was raised often, as it had been in the past. John Gardner, then President of the Carnegie Corporation, stated in 1955: "We send great numbers of our youth on to college each year without any clear notion as to what they will get out of it, but simply in pursuance of a vague notion that 'college is an opportunity that should not be denied them.' This makes no sense at all" (cited in Brown, 1955, p. 4). But the strong prevailing view was that the nation need not, would not, and could not afford to risk dividing up educational service instead of creating more. That educated men and women are the chief resource of America became an article of faith, a faith widely shared, even when the relationship of higher education to the health and prosperity of the nation was not measurable in specific terms. To procure expanded resources, then, would require expanded interpretation of the role of higher education in American society; many rallied to this cause who had not been previously involved.

The setting for the financial expansion between 1955 and 1970 was built upon public affirmation of the social benefits of expanded educational opportunity. The necessity for the achievement of this goal became a top national priority and, in a period of prosperity, higher education was at last able to compete with other public services for government and philanthropic assistance. Needs were never fully met, but the rising tide of enrolments was contained. Similarly, the rising tide of expectations from advanced education and research was an encouragement to other developments in education and service. But the effort to win public good will through better understanding of the role, nature, needs, and potential of higher education was a massive undertaking, the success of which was continuously measured in available funds. Competition was severe. Increasing population created demands for financial assistance in other areas of public service—new facilities and services for health care, recreation, social service, and elementary-secondary education; for new highways and public utilities; and other operations.

The consensus of task forces, observers, and analysts of the higher education scene as regards finance was that all previous sources of income would have to be expanded and new ones created. Multiple sources of support offered less danger of undue influence from any one source; and it was neither realistic nor practicable to expect that one source, not even the federal government, could or would carry the new load.

The private institutions naturally looked to traditional private giving. New approaches were necessary, however. Groups of institutions organized for joint effort under the sponsorship of state organizations or national committees. The Council on Financial Aid to Education was created for data gathering, counseling, and national advertising of higher education needs. Originally organized in the interests of private higher education, the council later came to encompass voluntary giving to public institutions.

State institutions also began to solicit gifts, primarily from alumni; private institutions in some states were openly critical of this policy. A most unfortunate, divisive and misleading argument was advanced by some spokesmen, primarily from the business world, that private giving should be directed exclusively to private institutions. These spokesmen claimed that private institutions were the educational prototype of free enterprise, whereas public institutions under government control were not free enterprise. The special tax status given to private institutions and to the gifts made to them as a reflection of the public nature of their service was seldom mentioned. Private education was in greater need, it was further claimed, because public institutions had recourse to public appropriations—suggesting that the needs of public universities were always fulfilled for the asking. Fortunately, these arguments now reflect the views of few private higher education leaders or their constituents, but they were influential in decisions made by corporations and many individuals for over a decade. After all such arguments, the view prevailed that all would benefit from an enlargement of total gifts and that many of the gifts to public universities would not necessarily go to the private institutions under different circumstances. As private institutions have come to seek public assistance, the old debate largely has become moot.

Voluntary giving was enlarged by corporate giving. Favorable court review of the practice opened the door, and increasing public acceptance of the concept of a corporate citizenship, with responsibilities beyond direct business operations, led to a variety of corporate plans. Total annual support through gifts from all sources, as reported by the Council for Financial Aid to Education, Inc. (1972), grew from $289,541,520 in 1954–55 to $1,244,815,734 in 1964–65. Although data for the years after 1965, allowing for inflation, reflect a plateau rather than growth—a condition associated with the general fiscal situation in the late sixties—private giving to higher education grew in importance for a decade and remains important.

The organization of affiliated foundations helped to increase financial resources from nontax sources in the public universities. Each foundation was established as a private corporation but with purposes limited to assisting the associated college or university. A foundation usually had a number of purposes. It could act as trustee for benefactions from donors who did not want to use an agency controlled by government. The foundation could borrow money for longer periods than was usually allowed at a public institution and the foundation could finance projects supported by student, auxiliary, or regular income. Many residence halls and student unions were financed in this manner, a significant service in the expansion of campus facilities. Recreation and physical education facilities were often similarly funded. A foundation could also undertake appropriate investments, a practice increasingly popular with a number of private institutions. In these cases, the boards of control were not restricted as were those in the public sector. Finally, the institutional foundations became the focal point for fund solicitation, both independently and in association with alumni organizations.

How to increase income from endowment and trust funds also became a subject of broad concern. The ultraconservative "conservator" concept, which greatly restricted the range of investments, gave way to the "prudent man" investment philosophy—a change induced by the business mood of the times and by the growing urgency of the need for additional income. For the same reasons, annual giving became more popular than increasing endowments.

Although the scramble for resources was productive, a huge deficit remained between need and reality. The steady increase in categorical assistance from the federal government pointed to the possibility of more such aid and the opening of new support channels from this source. Federal aid for higher education became the dominant theme on the agenda of academic planning.

J. L. Morrill (1955, p. 41), then president of the University of Minnesota, told a conference of the Academy of Political and Social Science: "Relationships of higher education with the federal government have become a major preoccupation in the American college and university world. They enter significantly into financing and policy. . . . The whole notion, indeed, of organized education as a social function—public and private—has assumed new political overtones."

# 8

## Sputnik, Science, and Support

The concept of federal assistance to colleges and universities was first reflected in federal land grants to territories and new states to encourage the establishment of seminaries, colleges, normal schools, schools of mines, and universities. The pragmatic immediate concern, however, was primarily to encourage land development. The precedent was broadened with the Morrill Act of 1862 and subsequent related legislation, but again the concern was as much a strengthened agriculture and industry as the higher education of students. By World War I, colleges and universities had become enough a part of the social establishment to merit both aid and attention through their recruitment for war purposes. World War II followed the same course. (Before the war was concluded, however, the contributions of colleges and universities were increasingly acknowledged to have been justified on their own merit as a basis for national action.)

The federal educational involvement in the Depression was aimed at welfare and economic relief, although again the results had educational significance and the system was thereby strengthened. The G.I. Bill had its chief support from concern with economic stability and the effects of possible unemployment, but the human dividends were great and higher education was strengthened by the experience.

It may be generalized that before the sixties funds from the federal government to colleges and universities were for specific federal purposes and services—student aid, research, training programs for federal departments, participation in overseas activity, officer education for the military and the education of specialized personnel for other departments, and consultation with academic specialists.

In spite of these and many other relationships over a period of more than one hundred years, a federal policy to assist higher education fulfill its primary purposes was not legislated until 1965. The many programs instituted for federal objectives greatly affected the course of higher education, but such programs were instituted for diverse and restricted objectives and administered by numerous federal agencies. Each program was a response to a federal need rather than a clear obligation or intent to assist higher education to fulfill its missions. Under law and precedent, higher education continued to be regarded as primarily a responsibility of the states.

## Reasons for Federal Education Policy

The Tidal Wave became a pressure point in this developing relationship, a crucial one. The data on capability versus enrolments indicated that even if former proportions of educational income could be sustained during the enrolment rise, substantially more help would be needed from the federal government. Without such assistance, loss of educational opportunity would become a political and social problem and the quality and effectiveness of the institutions would be diminished.

This view was by no means universally held. John Millet (1955, p. 210), who had directed the report of the Commission on Financing Higher Education, stated: "No interest at all has been aroused in the suggestion for general subvention by the federal government of state higher education, and there seems to be little demand for a national scholarship program. This situation should create cause for general thanksgiving, since general federal support could only lead to undesirable intervention in educational affairs." Perkins (1955, p. 108), President of the University of Delaware, did not see much prospect for increased federal assistance in any form under a budget-balancing administration and seemed more concerned over the danger of government control than the current financial stress. "It would be tragic to jeopardize higher education purely out of zeal to finance greater educational opportunity. If faced with the choice, we might better have less educational opportunity and maintain freedom."

Davidson (1955, pp. 118–122), President of Union College, a leader among private college heads, spoke against expanding federal involvement beyond the financing of programs "distinctly federal in nature and of direct assistance to the federal government, such as contract research and the rehabilitation of war veterans. There is a strong feeling that if we do not stick to this principle of programmatic aid, there will be no limit to the invasion of local autonomy by federal activities." Although skeptical of the need for a general federal scholarship program, Davidson acknowledged that 83 percent of the private colleges and 80 percent of the public approved the idea in a 1949 survey. However, Davidson thought the extension of the G.I. benefits for Korean veterans removed the urgency for action.

Even President Morrill, who believed the "increasing governmental relationships are an instance of inevitable logic" saw "danger signals." He regretted the institution by the Pentagon of "the obnoxious 'loyalty oath'" procedure for ROTC students; the Defense Department action to assert its right to dismiss employees under correspondence instruction contract for "security" reasons, without presenting evidence or opportunity for self-defense; and the failure of the government to provide full cost for research contracts. Morrill had confidence, however, that complexities of this kind were in the long run subject to mutually satisfactory "adjustment," although vigilance had to be continuously exercised (Morrill, 1955, pp. 42–45).

The pressure of the Tidal Wave greatly intensified when Russia's Sputnik orbited the earth in 1957. The fallout of concern from that event prevailed over the apprehensions and reservations about federal control, about the question of public assistance for private institutions, about the dangers of carrying mass higher education too far, about the intrusion of political forces beyond the formalities of government action. When Sputnik, the first man-made satellite to orbit the earth, was launched, the reaction in all circles was consternation, sometimes close to panic. Questions flew as to why Russian scientific capability appeared to be superior to that of the United States, and the questions centered on American education. Were enough scientists being trained, was the training of sufficient quality, was the public support of science adequate, did governmental and educational policies give sufficient emphasis to science? Russian education suddenly became a subject of great interest.

From the tradition of "Yankee ingenuity" to the atomic bomb, American scientific achievement had been taken for granted. Science and technology had come to be accepted as the keys to future progress—in industry, medicine, and agriculture. Now might we become dependent upon foreign science? Auburn, President of the University of Akron, pointed up this concern: "We well remember that we are indebted to German, Italian, and Danish scientists for the development of the atom bomb, and more recently of rockets and missiles. Where would we be today if Wernher von Braun, Edward Teller, or Ernest Steinhoff had decided to settle in another country? Where would we be if the Army's 'Operation Paperclip,' designed to bring West European scientists to this country, had failed" (1958, p. 17)?

A week after the Sputnik display, Murphy (1958, p. 35) captured the prevailing mood of the delegates to the annual meeting (1957) of the American Council on Education: "The message which this little ball carries to Americans, if they would but stop and listen, is that in the last half of the 20th century . . . nothing is as important as the trained and educated mind. This sphere . . . states more dramatically than ever before that the future of the 20th century lies in the hands of those

who have placed education and its Siamese twin—research—
in the position of priority."

The U.S. Commissioner of Education, Lawrence G. Der-
thick, reinforced the point, speaking for a group of American
educators who studied education in the Soviet Union in 1958:
"What we have seen has amazed us in one outstanding particular. . . . Everywhere we saw indication after indication of what
we could only conclude amounted to a total commitment to
education (cited in *Congressional Record,* August 13, 1958,
*104,* p. 15835).

Although Congress and the Administration in 1956 and
early 1957 were beginning to note the possible need for greater
federal support for higher education in response to the prospective Tidal Wave, action was slow to develop. Indeed, without
Sputnik the National Defense Education Act of 1958, inadequate as it was as an aid to institutions, might not have been
adopted, or at least not at that time.

Rivlin reminds us that when the House Committee on
Education and Labor began hearings on scholarship and
student loan fund legislation in the summer of 1957, the committee first sought the views of educators. When the correspond-
ing committee in the Senate opened similar hearings in January
1958, the first witnesses were scientists—all of whom were
asked to give their views on what was wrong with American
education! The Tidal Wave yielded to Sputnik as the center
of the focus (Rivlin, 1961, p. 73).

A great variety of proposals were made by witnesses before
the congressional committees, by resolutions of organizations,
and in editorial commentary. The areas most frequently mentioned were the need for giving greater emphasis to science in
the high school; the need to upgrade the quality of instruction
in both high school and college; the need to encourage able and
talented high school graduates to go to college; the need to assist
college students with scholarships, loan funds, and fellowships;
and the need for adequate instructional facilities. "During 1957
and 1958, members of the 85th Congress introduced about 1500
bills affecting education, and the Congress enacted at least 80

laws involving education in some way" (Quattlebaum, 1960, p. 31).

The intangible results of the public concern were also evident. "Everywhere standards of performance were raised, and actual course requirements were made tougher" (Veysey, 1973, p. 16). The same attitude prevailed at the high school level. Even before Sputnik, a good deal of dissatisfaction had been expressed with the preparation of secondary school students for college work. De Kiewiet (1955, p. 3), President of the University of Rochester, referred to the "damaging" and "useless" controversy that "has raged about the manner in which the high school system of the country fails to provide adequate preparation for college and university." In the aftermath of Sputnik, the critics were reinforced.

It was fortuitous that the recommendations of the President's Committee on Education Beyond the High School were at hand as Congress reached for an action program. The committee issued its major report in July 1957. Six months later, Congress was searching for answers as to how to enlarge and improve higher education. The committee had five central proposals for the federal agenda. All of them could be related to the concerns generated by Sputnik as well as by the Tidal Wave, for the concerns had become inseparable: aid for the construction of college and university facilities through grants and loan funds; aid to students through scholarships, loan funds, work-study programs, and tax deductions or credits to parents or students; assistance to graduate schools through fellowships and direct grants; aid to institutions as supplements to scholarships and fellowships; reorganization of federal relations to centralize, improve, and enlarge data-gathering and to evaluate and coordinate the multiple federal programs related to higher education.

## Federal Programs and Support

In varying degrees and different ways, these recommendations except for the last were put into effect over a period of time. The National Defense Education Act of September 2, 1958, especially, was a landmark piece of legislation. The law authorized diverse channels for federal assistance to higher education, most of which were later encompassed in the program underlying the Higher Education Act of 1965. The NDEA provided for student loans (with a "forgiveness" feature for elementary-secondary teachers), fellowships for advanced study (with special provision for students of modern languages), aid for language and area centers, for advanced study institutes, for counseling and guidance institutes, and for grants to states for counseling and testing programs in elementary-secondary schools and junior colleges. (Paralleling the NDEA provisions, grants for fellowships from the National Institutes of Health—a program which had started with the National Cancer Institute in the thirties—grew in number and expanded to include trainees and trainee programs. NIH awards in 1960 totaled 3,723, and comparable programs were sponsored by the Atomic Energy Commission and the National Science Foundation.)

The National Defense Education Act was obviously piecemeal legislation. Financially, its assistance to operations was indirect and the benefits were spread unevenly among institutions. Some educators had hoped for general financial assistance that would not be tied to student aid or to the special programs selected. But no such over-all program had been placed before the Congress, and no such plan had a consensus among the higher education institutions. Even within categories of expenditures, more meaningful assistance could have been channelled to housing, payment for ROTC facilities, for full administrative costs in contract research and training programs, and teaching facilities in medicine and a variety of other fields. These examples would probably have had a higher priority than student aid as new avenues for funding.

Nevertheless, the National Defense Education Act was a point of departure in the emerging role of the federal government in higher education. As with earlier programs, a "defense" tag was attached to link the program to the traditional literal application of "federal" interests, but the effect of the legislation was a clear recognition that aiding students promotes the general welfare. The intent "clearly was to use federal resources to strengthen higher education generally. This recognition of higher education as a national concern may well turn out to be the most important feature of the Act" (Rivlin, 1961, p. 119).

Perhaps the major single effect of Sputnik on higher education was acceleration of research and the provision of increased funding for this purpose by the federal government; state and private resources also increased assistance. The teacher and scholar had always believed that intellectual inquiry was part of his role, but new pressure was added for research done under contract or grants for the federal government or for industry.

The growth of academic research and its influential interaction with graduate work and the undergraduate curricula had preceded Sputnik. Academic men of science, and to a more limited extent professors in other disciplines, were emphasizing even in the twenties the importance of basic research. Conant believes that had the Depression and World War II not convulsed higher education in the thirties and forties, "revolutionary changes in the support of university departments of science would have occurred. What we have seen in the 1950s and 1960s, I regard as a postponed logical continuation of what was just starting before the great depression" (1970, p. 78).

During the war, academic science had established its importance in national defense and technology in ways not to be forgotten, and research policy was being formulated by accretion even before government policy for higher education itself received conscious attention. "The war created a need for highly sophisticated scientific manpower and knowledge. University scientists were quick to respond and produced spectacular results. After the war, the *ad hoc* wartime arrangements were modified and institutionalized to ensure the continuation of scientific research required for defense and for an expanding series of civilian needs" (National Board on Graduate Education, 1974, p. 15).

The National Science Foundation was established in 1950. It did not supplant other agencies in granting research funds nor did it have authority to coordinate research interests of the government; but it was and continues to be particularly interested in strengthening the research capability of the universities. By 1955, research was an acknowledged "preoccupation of higher education." Stoke, then dean of the Graduate School at the University of Washington, claimed, "Research activities in our colleges and universities have reached almost feverish proportions, with marked effect upon curricula development" (1955, p. 61).

The rapid expansion of government support for university health research was another important postwar development. Most of the funds were channeled through the National Institutes of Health. The Department of Defense, the Atomic Energy Commission, the Department of Health, Education and Welfare (of which NIH was a part), the Department of Agriculture, and (beginning in 1958) the National Aeronautics and Space Administration were other major departments granting or contracting for funds to universities (Rivlin, 1961, p. 38).

The most obvious response to Sputnik was the creation and rapid growth of the National Aeronautics and Space Administration. However, each of the major mission-oriented federal agencies continued to increase its funding of basic research as a proportion of over-all allocations to research and development. Between 1963 and 1972, federal support of basic research at universities and colleges increased from $610 million to $1,409 million.[1] Translated to constant dollars, the spread is not so great but still represents an impressive development in higher education within a relatively short period (National Board on Graduate Education, 1974, p. 17). In the same period, the expenditures of the universities from institutional funds for basic research in constant dollars rose by 59 percent and continued to increase even after federal expenditures leveled off.

From about 1958, the education of highly trained manpower for university research and teaching and for research work in other areas also received national attention. As a result, large federal sums were made available for fellowships and traineeships, research assistantships, and training grants. Some institutional aid accompanied the grants. Loan funds and work-

[1] In 1939, university research expenditures from all sources was $27 million (Pusey, 1963, p. 161); in 1959, $356 million; in 1960, federal funds for research and development at educational institutions was $464 million (Rivlin, 1961, p. 35).

study opportunities for graduate students were established. A number of federal departments were involved, and by 1968 51,400 graduate students were supported on fellowships and traineeships—more than triple in a five-year period. (This figure does not include NIH-NIHM training grants or research assistantships.) The humanities and social sciences were included among the research areas (National Board on Graduate Education, 1974, pp. 18–21).

As distinguished from restricted or project aid, general institutional aid from the federal government continued to be debated throughout the period. The organizations of colleges and universities had difficulty in agreeing on a single program, but nearly all had come to a recognition of the need for federal assistance in dealing with the new numbers and enlarged functions. This was true particularly in professional and graduate education and in research. As the debate on federal aid continued, institutional funding to supplement local resources came from cost-of-education allowances associated with fellowships, traineeships, and tuition payments for training grants; from National Institutes of Health and National Science Foundation research supplement grants; from NSF general program support; and from grants for Research and Development and facility construction grants.

This inadequate piecemeal approach to aid to institutions was often deplored. The institutional benefits of the National Defense Education Act of 1958 were indirect and uneven. It was clear, however, that the major reason the Congress had not undertaken sweeping new programs for colleges and universities was the absence of an integrated plan supported by all important elements in higher education. The doctrinaire debate over federal aid as well as over the appropriate means would go on as a consensus too slowly developed. Such consensus finally found partial expression in the Educational Facilities Act of 1963, the first step toward a more comprehensive program of institutional assistance.

The risks and dangers from federal financial involvement in higher education were analyzed many times (Pusey, 1963). In considering large scale research fundings, Kerr has pointed to federal "influence" if not control on institutional decision making; to loss of institutional autonomy through separate budgeting for specific purposes, often negotiated by project directors outside normal procedures; to inflexibility in the distribution of funds; to external pressures for exceptions to established institutional policies; to imbalances among the disciplines; to uneven distribution of resources among institutions; to the growth of nonteaching personnel and activities; and to new administrative burdens, including additional institutional costs. Kerr nonetheless concluded, "With all its problems, however, federal research aid to universities has helped greatly in meeting national needs. It has greatly assisted the universities themselves. The nation is stronger. The leading universities are stronger" (1972, p. 68). Most presidents of federal grant-receiving universities regarded federal aid as a "good thing" (Orlans, 1962, p. 9) and the institutions quickly and effectively adapted to their new role.

Throughout the discussions with Congress and in organizational actions, that basic institutional support would continue to be the responsibility of the states and private sources was taken for granted. But the case for the federal government to share in that responsibility was now generally accepted in the academic community and was coming to be accepted within the government. Federal assistance should apply not only to research, construction, student aid, and ad hoc programs but also to basic operations. Basic operations particularly concerned community colleges, and colleges and universities not heavily involved in research. Federal aid had come a long way, but it was time for a policy definition.

## Changing Federal Policy

Thus, the most notable, and perhaps the most important, single subject in the record of higher education in the sixties was the search for ways and means whereby the federal government could appropriately and effectively assist colleges and universities in carrying out responsibilities clearly related to the national interest.

By 1960, many federal actions had affected educational progress, beginning with events in the late 18th century described in previous chapters. The point has been made that the federal government, in the absence of a well-defined and clearly formulated policy toward higher education (other than regarding it as a private or state government responsibility), cloaked each action within a targeted federal purpose. Sometimes the format was the purchase of services, such as contract research or training for government employees; sometimes it was the fulfilling of a federal obligation, as with the G.I. educational benefits; sometimes it was the rendering of services in solving a predetermined national problem—land development, unemployment, war training, welfare activity.

As indicated earlier, the National Defense Education Act of 1958 contained a suggestion of a new approach. It included a directive to the Secretary of Health, Education and Welfare to "Advise and consult with the heads of departments and agencies . . . responsible for the administration of scholarships, fellowships, or other educational programs with a view to securing full information concerning all specialized scholarships, fellowships, or other educational programs administered by or under any such department or agency and to developing policies and procedures *which will strengthen the educational programs and objectives of the institutions of higher education utilized for such purposes* by any such department or agency" (*Congressional Record,* August 21, 1958, *104,* p. 17507, emphasis added).

John F. Kennedy was the first president to state formally the case for a recognition of higher education as a federal concern. President Kennedy said in his education message to the Congress in January 1963:

> Education is the keystone in the arch of freedom and progress. Nothing has contributed more to the enlargement of this nation's strength and opportunities than our traditional system of free, universal elementary and secondary education, coupled with widespread availability of college education. . . .
>
> For the nation, increasing the quality and avail-

ability of education is vital to both our national
security and our domestic well-being. . . .

This nation is committed to greater investment
in economic growth; and recent research has shown
that one of the most beneficial of all such investments
is education, accounting for some 40 percent of the
nation's growth and productivity in recent years. . . .

In the new age of science and space, improved
education is essential to give new meaning to our national purpose and power. . . .

In short, from every point of view, education is
of paramount concern to the national interest as well
as to each individual. . . .

The proper federal role is to identify national
education goals and to help local, state, and private
authorities build the necessary roads to reach those
goals.

The goals included improving the quality and quantity of
instruction in schools and colleges and "increasing opportunities and incentives for all Americans to develop their talents to
the utmost." The guidelines were an appraisal of "the entire
range of educational problems," including graduate education
and continuing education; selective application of federal aid
"aimed at strengthening" the system and meeting urgent problems, including manpower shortages, the need for improved educational facilities, and a "more effective implementation of
existing laws."

The message accompanied a single comprehensive education bill, proposed as the National Education Improvement
Act of 1963. The bill dealt with expansion of student assistance,
including graduate fellowships, loan funds, and work-study opportunities; expansion and improvement of higher education
facilities through loans and grants; program grants in fields of
anticipated manpower shortages, including language and area
centers; grants for library materials and construction; expansion of graduate education and research in all fields, including
increased numbers of graduate centers. Emphasis was given spe-

cifically to research in education and to the establishment of centers for multipurpose educational research; development and demonstration programs; and training institutes to upgrade knowledge and skills of teachers. Special sections dealt with elementary and secondary education and continuing education.

President Kennedy's message concluded with the comment that the bill, if enacted, would encourage "the increase of the knowledge, skills, attitudes, and critical intelligence necessary for the preservation of our society. It will help keep America strong and safe and free."

Congressional action did not follow the omnibus education form recommended, but the many specific actions taken in 1963–64 reflected the new stance. Particularly important, apart from student assistance and research funding, were the Higher Education Facilities Act of 1963, the Health Professions Educational Assistance Act of 1963, amendments in 1963 to the National Defense Education Act, the Library Services and Construction Act of 1964, the Economic Opportunity Act of 1964, and the Foreign Assistance Act of 1964. More than 30 other bills enacted in this period were related to new or enlarged educational activity. President Johnson's message to Congress in January 1965 urged "that we push ahead with the number one business of the American people—the education of our youth in preschools, elementary and secondary schools, and in the colleges and universities" (Quattlebaum, 1968, P. 1, p. 42).

The Eighty-Ninth Congress (1965–66) continued the pace. The Higher Education Act of 1965 (the first legislation with such a comprehensive title) authorized appropriations for aiding community educational services and continuing education programs, increasing college library resources, and strengthening developing colleges. In separate bills, a breakthrough was achieved in aid to colleges in the health sciences—for programs, scholarships and facilities—and for the allied health professions. The National Foundation for the Arts and Humanities was established in 1965. The list of Congressional actions was a long one, and President Johnson remarked upon signing the Higher Education Act of 1965: "This bill is only one of more than two dozen education measures enacted by the first session of the

Eighty-Ninth Congress. And history will forever record that this session . . . did more for the wonderful cause of education in America than all the previous 176 regular sessions of Congress did, put together" (Quattlebaum, 1968, Pt. 1, p. 42).

The change in attitude toward, priority for, and philosophy of federal involvement in higher education that had developed in the period between 1958 and 1968 was clearly reflected by President Johnson in his message to Congress on February 5, 1968 (quoted in Burns, 1968, pp. 409–414):

> The prosperity and well-being of the United States—and thus our national interest—are vitally affected by America's colleges and universities, junior colleges, and technical institutes.
>
> Their problems are not theirs alone, but the Nation's.
>
> This is true today more than ever. For now we call upon higher education to play a new and more ambitious role in our social progress, our economic development, our efforts to help other countries.
>
> We depend upon universities—their training, research and extension services—for the knowledge which undergirds agricultural and industrial production.
>
> Increasingly, we look to the colleges and universities—to their faculties, laboratories, research institutes, and study centers—for help with every problem in our society and with the efforts we are making toward peace in the world. . . .
>
> Today, higher education needs help.
>
> American colleges and universities face growing enrollments, rising costs, and increasing demands for services of all kinds. . . .
>
> The programs I am presenting to the Congress today are aimed at solving some of the problems faced by our colleges and universities and their students in the years ahead. But accomplishing all these things will by no means solve the problems of higher education in America.

To do that, we must shape a long-term strategy of Federal aid to higher education: a comprehensive set of goals and a precise plan of action.

I am directing the Secretary of Health, Education and Welfare to begin preparing a long-range plan for the support of higher education in America.

Our strategy must eliminate race and income as bars to higher learning; guard the independence of private and public institutions; ensure that state and private contributions will bear their fair share of support for higher education; encourage the efficient and effective use of educational resources by our colleges and universities; promote continuing improvement in the quality of American education; effectively blend support to students with support for institutions.

Such a strategy will not be easy to devise. But we must begin now. For at stake is a decision of vital importance to all Americans.

While the new level of federal involvement undoubtedly made the higher education system more useful to the nation in the ways indicated by President Johnson and anticipated by President Kennedy, congressional action did not deal with the issue of greatest concern to the greatest number of colleges and universities—assisting institutions generally in meeting the financial requirements of their basic operations.

Aid to students is not always or necessarily aid to institutions. Student aid has always been good for the nation in enhancing educational opportunity, although in some instances financial assistance to students subsidized geographical mobility rather than opportunity. But the institutions would have been overcrowded in the sixties without the student aid programs. Where student aid allowed institutions to divert traditional resources for that purpose to other uses, federal aid provided institutional assistance indirectly. Also, when student aid made possible a higher level of tuition and other charges, it had a bearing on institutional support—but this point could not be pressed without defeating the direct and avowed purpose of the legislation.

Similarly, aid to research was not necessarily operational aid; such funding enabled institutions to enlarge and improve their research programs and the returns were undeniably valuable to the nation. But significant help for over-all institutional finance was received only when "cost-of-education" allowances for graduate students were a part of the projects, and such projects affected a small proportion of the total number. There were times, furthermore, when indirect costs of federal projects were not fully funded. Institutions were in fact often financially worse off than they would have been without the contract or grant. Further, when a grant or contract was not renewed, the institutions had to bear the reconversion expense.

Grants for educational facilities were clearly direct and helpful aid, relieving capital budgets, but they were one-time rather than continuing assistance. If the institution did not plan conservatively, it was left with an enlarged plant maintenance and operation obligation that cut into other available resources. The program grants were clearly a net financial gain if the institution was already engaged in the activity, such as library service. If the grant induced program expansion, however, additional resources on a continuing basis had to be acquired.

From the point of view of institutional stability, educators expressed disappointment that so many new ventures were authorized while old obligations were bypassed. Funds were provided for new centers of excellence in research and graduate training, while the established centers were not always included on the same basis. Also, newly subsidized programs generated new enrolments, for which space and basic services had to be provided from other sources.

Clearly, the basic needs of higher education generally had not been met and remained a challenge to the federal government as well as to other sources of support. The Carnegie Commission on Higher Education (1968, p. 8) based its report on new levels of federal responsibility for higher education on this consideration. Growth in numbers, in functions, and increasing costs due to inflation required immediate attention: "The Carnegie Commission believes a much greater federal investment is now essential if the growth of higher education is not to be curbed at the very time that the national need is so crucial for our best ideas and intellectual skills and for the broadest possible extension of equality of opportunity."

In spite of the new rhetoric, the new legislation, and the accelerated spending, the government had not found a way to provide general assistance that would be equitable, helpful in meeting primary needs, and reliable in continuing financing. President Johnson was sensitive and wise in saying that building a strategy for the long-range support of higher education would not be easy. The president might have added that the political prospects for success were not encouraged by the inability of the higher education leaders to form a consensus on an across-the-board institutional assistance program. Nor was the education establishment encouraged by the failure of the Congress to fund fully the activities it had previously authorized. Many programs that had been passed lagged in time and funding. The International Education Act, for example, was never funded.

The significance of the failure to devise specific continuing policy was reflected in the years after 1968. In fact, the drastic changes in direction and funding contributed to a "new depression" in higher education. As a new presidential administration changed goals and priorities, federal support in a number of areas declined or was eliminated. Indeed, such fluctuations operated independently of changes in law or statements of purpose. Obviously, what had happened in the decade was not built upon firm, clear, or continuing policy. Institutions had to adjust as best they could.

# 9

# Priority Lost

The chronicle of higher education in the decade 1958–1968 was one of unprecedented enrolment growth, expansion of programs, and increase in functions. Institutions were responsive to the social demand for new services, increased research productivity, and improved educational opportunity. The financial requirements for this response were supported by the high level of public confidence. The public regarded higher education as essential to economic growth, national defense, social gain, and equality of opportunity in employment and in fulfilling individual cultural and social aspirations.

In this environment, although basic operations were not funded at a level to justify current references to "affluence" and "the golden years," faculty salaries were brought to an appropriate peer relationship among the professions for the first time in the history of higher education. At the same time, the lag in facilities and internal supporting services was fairly well overcome. "The schools were forced to scramble for funds, but they managed to make ends meet" (Cheit, 1971, p. 1). The institutions also managed to improve the quality of their performance while extending the scope of their activities.

About 1968, it became apparent that the cost trend induced by the growth period exceeded income prospects. In 1971, Cheit wrote in *The New Depression in Higher Education* that institutional reports, articles by analysts, and front page news stories on "the money problem of colleges and universities" began to appear and that by 1970, "nearly every popular journal

. . . recognized that higher education was in a financial depression" and had published "its 'financial-crisis-on-the-campus' article." Cheit continued: "After a decade of building, expanding, and undertaking new responsibilities, the trend on campuses today is all in the other direction. The talk, the planning, and the decisions now center on reallocating, on adding only by substitution, on cutting, trimming, even struggling to hang on. Just a few years ago, the main assignment of a new college or university president was to develop plans for building the institution. Today's new president is more likely to find financial conditions dictate that his first priority is to scale down his school's plans and, perhaps, even its operation" (Cheit, 1971, p. 3).

The downturn in the financial condition may be traced to a number of reasons. The unexpected acceleration in the general inflation rate magnified costs, and dollars bought less. Federal resources that had gone to institutional income declined as a proportion of educational expenditures; unsettled economic conditions affected income from endowment and gifts; and tuition income could not be significantly increased without diminishing returns or incurring political opposition or both. What increases there were in public appropriations were often earmarked for community colleges or programs in the health sciences, including medicine. Capital expenditures followed the same course.[1]

The downturn not only came suddenly, but because it emanated from all sources simultaneously and sharply there

[1] The largest element in the increased support of higher education basic operations in the sixties was in state appropriations. The figures compiled by the Carnegie Commission on Higher Education (1973, pp. 148–161) estimate aggregate state appropriations for 1957–58 to have been approximately $1.15 billion and in 1969–70 $5.95 billion, an increase of more than 500 percent. These estimates must be interpreted as over-all indices, however, and not as reflecting precise conditions in any single state. Further, because states differ in their classification of expenditures, comparisons should not be drawn among segments of higher education service or as regards so-called "per student expenditures." Also, state practices in support of private higher education vary greatly, from none at all except tax exemptions, to large tuition grants, to direct assistance.

The conclusion may be drawn, however, that the chief burden of was little opportunity for gradual adjustment. In some states, the curtailments moved quickly from cuts in requests to cuts in expenditures when computed in constant dollars. The result in many instances was harsher treatment for higher education than for most of the economy and other areas of public service. Further, the cutback was more damaging to senior baccalaureate and graduate institutions than to community colleges and student aid. Obviously, the priority for higher education had changed.

The experience of one major state university demonstrates the changed environment at the end of the short period of high priority (1958–1968). In Illinois, the governor in 1960 regretfully said that while not all budget requests could be met, the state did the best it possibly could considering total state income and obligations. In 1969, the governor's state budget bureau asserted (without discussion) not only that the request of the university was disallowed, but that even if the state had more funds to allocate they would not go to the university. Support of higher education institutionally had been good politics in 1960; apparently, it was not good politics in 1970. A similar view was expressed by budget-makers at the national level, both in the executive departments and in Congress.

Every observer, analyst, critic, and professional participant has his own "bill of particulars" as to what happened to the priority for higher education. They range from a general condemnation of federal involvement to disavowal of mass attendance as public policy; from an assertion of misdirected purposes and goals to a charge that egalitarianism has affected standards with a consequent loss of respect. Unfortunately, most of the analytical commentary is subjective. Time has been too brief for adequate research fully to substantiate opinions, positive or negative, on cause and effect.

There can be no doubt that the loss of priority is related to

---

servicing the expansion in enrolments and in programs fell upon local resources, state and private, including gifts and student payments. That federal, state, and local cutbacks were concurrent made the situation the more critical, with too little time for readjustment.

a lack of public confidence as to the importance of supporting higher education. Many of the contributing reasons for the shift in public attitude may be identified; some of these reasons existed in other periods, as we have noted earlier.

The first example that comes to mind is the public revulsion at the violence that characterized the years of student protest, particularly from 1964 to 1970. Although incidents were never as widespread as the public believed, since they were continually overexposed in the mass media, the violence was serious enough to justify public concern at all levels. A presidential study commission was appointed, the Carnegie Commission took note, speeches in the *Congressional Record* were numerous, social psychiatrists published widely, legislatures resolved and sometimes enacted, editorials were abundant, and books and journals as well as radio and television dealt exhaustively with student protest.

When dissent was peacefully expressed, it became tolerable if not commonly understood. Protest took forms unprecedented in the campus setting, but picket lines, strikes, demagogic harangues, and street demonstrations were sufficiently characteristic of the American scene that they were grudgingly accepted as permissible if not becoming, in an education community. But violence would not be tolerated and the inability of the institutions to substitute other methods for police and court action was not and is not yet appreciated fully. Institutions appeared inept in dealing with destruction and unwilling to use such authority as they had; they were circumscribed by court decisions regarding due process and restrained by student and faculty sentiment as well as by insufficient security procedures and resources. Public confidence in the management of institutions as well as in students and faculties generally was shaken. Backlash was inevitable and the full cost will not soon, if ever, be known. The image of the college or university as a symbol of objectivity in inquiry, rationality in discourse, and civility in human relations could not be reconciled with campus violence; instances of institutional paralysis on such occasions was beyond comprehension.

Curbstone critics as well as professional analysts were often wrong about what corrective measures were legally and practically possible in mob control and in individual discipline. Institutions were on the defensive and many questions remain unanswered. The indignities, disruptions, and lack of propriety aroused no sympathy for the harassed faculty and administration; an image of inadequate management appeared confirmed.

Whether student opinion of the main issue stemmed from the alienation of the members of the counterculture, widespread opposition to government Vietnam war policy or social philosophy, educational "reform," or general discontent and uncertainty about goals for the country as a whole, the institutions appeared to have failed in their responsibilities. The erosion of public confidence and, as a corollary, of public support was inevitable. The effect remains in unacknowledged ways: "The peculiar indignities suffered by many within academic institutions half a decade ago continue to fester. . . ." (Graubard, 1974, p. viii).

Some of the causal conditions to be identified transcend the educational scene, and first among these is a seeming general disenchantment with the Establishment. A 1972 Harris poll was reported (*Chicago Tribune,* July 13, 1972) as follows:

In the public and private sector, the Establishment is under heavy attack. Since 1966, public confidence in business leaders has slipped from 55 to 27 percent, while at the same time respect for the Supreme Court has dropped from 51 to 19 percent, for the executive branch of government from 41 to 19 percent, for the military from 62 to 24 percent.

This disenchantment with the Establishment has produced an accelerated sense of alienation among the voters, up from 40 to 47 percent in the last year. For example, the feeling that "what you think doesn't count much" has increased from 44 to 53 percent since 1971, and the concern that "people who have power are out to take advantage of you" has gone up from 33 to 38 percent in the last 12 months.

This mood finds its most visible manifestation in the issue of tax reform. By a nearly unanimous 90 to 96 percent, voters favor "tax reform with higher taxes for upper-income people." A substantial 74 percent of the voters feel "the tax laws were written to help the rich, not the average man."

It is reasonable to assume that anti-Establishment sentiment encompasses higher education. As a system, educational institutions are structured into the purposes and mechanisms of society and come within the purview of general social and political attitudes.

Economic insecurity looms large in recent public attitudes. Worry over inflation, trends in living costs, level of government expenditures and taxes have induced a mood of limited confidence in the immediate economic future. Apprehension that the economic and political world may be unmanageable has encouraged resistance to public expenditures except for military, welfare, and social service purposes. This resistance leaves little room for discriminatory judgments about the long-term strength and stability of institutions.[2]

Higher education is caught in the crisis of confidence in the economic future. "What seems to have happened in the last few years is that the burden of proof of the value of educational financing has shifted. The fact of a request is not enough" (Cheit, 1971, p. 155). "The fact of a request" never has been enough in the arduous business of resource acquisition, but there is a vast difference between interpreting the fact to a sympathetic audience and a doubting one!

In every period of stress, a plea has gone out from the aca-

[2] In Cheit's study of 41 institutions, an average expenditure growth was reported of 5 percent per student per year for the period 1969–70 to 1972–73. During that same period, the average annual increase in the consumer price index was 4.5. "Thus the difference was a remarkably small 0.5, or one-half of one percentage point above the increase in the consumer price index. . . . Given the findings of previous studies, this level of operation cannot continue for a very long period without serious adverse consequences to some of the institutions" (Cheit, 1973, pp. 53, 55).

demic community for greater public understanding. The failure to achieve such understanding is an underlying factor in the present condition, and how to achieve understanding for priority setting is bewildering. Some educators would formulate unifying themes in a search for consensus. But the broad purposes commonly given lip service—teaching, research, and public service—do not always have meaningful penetration into personal interests.

The average person has no clear perception of what the university as a whole, with all of its outreach, means to society. The public is only vaguely aware that society has some needs that only advanced learning can fulfill. People respect and want trained professionals in business, medicine, teaching, and other professions. The public wants the new ideas of research translated into technology and harnessed for the convenience and well-being of the community, and they sense that new ideas born in university research laboratories bear upon the quality of life. People respect the tradition of upward mobility in a democratic society. They know that dividing lines are inevitable in the human condition, and they are aware that education has provided the means for people to cross lines that in other societies would have restrained them into caste or class. They understand generally, if not in detail, that the system of higher education is related intimately to the economy, public leadership, and cultural achievements. But people do not recognize the value of the university whole nor understand fully the financial crisis that threatens effective university operations and future capabilities. Within this communication gap, in a period of stress, the priority of education has been so altered that institutions now face the prospect of receiving the leftovers after other needs are fulfilled—or at least more sympathetically considered.

The average person has his own ideas about priorities, and they are related to his own interests or knowledge. Hortatory generalizations do not add much to his understanding or conviction. When he moves from faith in the enterprise as a whole to evaluating specifics, his guidelines are his own limited experiences and contacts—student admissions; adequate professional care by doctor, lawyer, or teacher, for example; parental concern for opportunity; the means of his own career preparation or improvement; and personal relations with students, teachers, and other institutional personnel. With such subjective focus, the person cannot understand priorities involved in "a web of services" and activities that he does not know about or is not directly related to his experience. "It is an unhappy irony that the expansion in higher education that inevitably followed a great expansion in public support and public involvement has helped to undermine higher education. It demonstrated the delicacy of the interaction between educational leadership and the public's support" (Cheit, 1971, p. 156). The competing demands for support within higher education as well as between higher education and the other agencies of public service are bewildering and beyond the capability of the layman to reconcile. "Higher education lacks unity. This is a virtue, for it is a result of the great diversity of endeavors and it allows for many pluralistic initiatives. But it also has its costs. . . . Higher education is only loosely held together. The coming struggle for survival may demonstrate how loosely" (Kerr, 1975, p. 2).

Furthermore, in public affairs decision-making at the national, state, or local level, it is almost impossible to get separate or independent public reaction to issues of educational support. Except in an occasional bond issue, educational topics are inevitably entwined with other political and social concerns.

The politics of higher education must be considered in discussing the lost priority. During the early sixties, the gains were the outcome of public faith in the inherent value of the total enterprise. This faith was given substance by public awareness of how higher education related to such highly publicized issues as national defense and the importance of science and technology in a space age. Education potentially could contribute to the solution of problems that were pressing social concerns— urban affairs, poverty, crime, race relations, industrial and business expansion, professional needs, environmental control, and public management.

With the economic slowdown, complicated by inflation, competing demands for public support became the subject of political action at all levels. Historically, higher education has been dependent upon long-term public good will as contrasted with short-term political action. In political activity, higher education has no interest group to fight its battles and it is not well organized to fight its own. Defense, welfare, transportation, unemployment, crime prevention, health care, and other public services have been given precedence in public concern.

In an analysis of "The Politics of Higher Education," Moynihan (1975, p. 131) asserts that from the beginning and throughout the period of federal involvement, higher education "remained a passive force, acted upon rather than acting. No campaigns were organized; no great battles occurred; hardly any spokesmen emerged." The last comment could be successfully contradicted, but the general point remains. Moynihan continues: "In the 1950s and then in the 1960s initiatives concerning higher education arose primarily from the political interests and objectives of successive presidents and their administrations" (1975, p. 139).

Millett holds the same point of view with reference to state politics: "These observations lead . . . to the question about just what political resources a state university enjoys. I have asked myself this question for over twenty years, and I still do not have a satisfactory answer. The only answer I have is that a state university has such political resources as public good will affords. . . . State universities are not effective developers of political power." Millett later states: "The political process itself is little understood or appreciated by academic personnel, including students, faculties, and administrators. But even more important than the process itself is the relationship of the higher education community to the process. And here the record is especially dismal" (1974, pp. 29, 39, 142).

Whether political inadequacy is a failure of the system or an inevitable condition is a continuing question. That higher education has not been able to compete effectively for public support at a time of limited resources is widely acknowledged and substantiated by fiscal data.

As higher education has become more visible—because of growth, cost, and involvement in all aspects of life—institutions have become the subject of greater public discussion. The mass media, public forums, public opinion specialists, students, ministers, faculty members, and politicians continue to have their say. Some of the external commentary has been grossly misinformed; some of it has, as a result, been unwittingly distorted. How much such negative criticism has contributed to the diminishing public confidence cannot be measured. That such misinformation has had serious effect in this day of instant communication can be substantiated by any experienced college or university administrator. Unsupported allegations are often repeated until they are accepted as fact and become a part of the "literature" on higher education.

Although unpublished or unsupported criticism is sometimes best ignored, there are times when strategies should be planned for response. Such strategies apply particularly at the local or state level where the issues do not receive the attention of task forces, special committees, individual scholars, journals, or national occasions for analysis. Every state needs a blue-ribbon forum for high-level debate and discussion. The forum should include data gathering on important issues, now that governing boards are seen as advocates allegedly unconcerned with the broad public interest and coordinating boards tend to become instruments of state administration. At the state level, institutions desperately need unbiased, apolitical, professional mechanisms with high public visibility for disinterested and dispassionate hearings on issues of public concern (Henry, 1972, p. 288).

The alleged inadequacies in the governance of higher education were not confined to student life and campus behavior. "Accountability" became a new theme, especially popular with budget bureaus, legislators, and investigative reporters. The term often was used ambiguously. More often than not, the call for accountability has come from those who would spend less and who would like to dictate the ways and means to that end. Others would apply empirical standards to the essentially immeasurable—quality, intellectual growth, personal development, educational values. The search for comparable uniform costs or productivity standards is equally unfruitful. There are educational benefits as well as costs to be assessed and the techniques have not been formulated. Mandatory and rigid enforcement of inapplicable procedures are costly in red tape, damaging to morale, and lead to inefficiency. Incremental experience has a value not to be carelessly discarded.

However, the reality of today's world will allow no return to the code of other days, which governed the formal external relationships of colleges and universities. Administrative officers must face the inevitability of adversary relationships with coordinating boards, governors, legislatures, courts, and the federal government, in addition to accrediting agencies, and professional organizations. The adversary relationship also exists for people without mandate who presume to speak for the public: editors, commentators, and self-appointed spokesmen for higher education.

Nonetheless, computerized "inputs" and "outputs" are useful tools in many aspects of institutional management and are not to be brushed aside by resisting consideration of how to take advantage of new approaches (Balderston, 1974, pp. 140, 159, 177, 247). Finding a balance between external regulation and "the efficiency of freedom" will be an effort essential to future public confidence.

Confusion over enrolment trends has contributed to the external insistence upon "accountability." Decline in the *rate* of increase (much lower than the earlier projections) often has been generalized into "declining enrolments." The implications for revising capital plans are clear, but the requirements for funding additional enrolments, even at a lower rate, have not been fully appreciated. As a result, per student support in many institutions has actually declined (discounting inflation), resulting in inadequate salary adjustments, postponed maintenance, and one-time savings that sometimes are woven into base levels of ongoing support. Higher education is not in "steady state," Glenny (1974, p. 25) has forcefully pointed out.

"The fact is that the age group of 18–21-year olds, the primary source of undergraduate students, has continued to increase at a rather substantial rate." The number will steadily increase during the 1970s. Institutional generalizations are difficult, however, because conditions vary by regions, types of institutions, programs, and nature of student body. "Instability" is a more appropriate description than "equilibrium" (Glenny, 1974, p. 25).

The recession view of the value of the college degree in the job market has also been a factor in the public reaction to supporting either growth or the present level of enrolment. Most educators deplore an exclusive emphasis on a dollar evaluation of a college education, but student and family interest in vocations and professions have been a dominant influence in enrolment growth.

Long-term career preparation remains an important motivation for college attendance. Relating career decisions to the immediate market, however, can be unfortunate both for the individual and the system, particularly when the decision on college attendance is at stake. The recent publicity campaign of the U.S. Office of Education, emphasizing that many careers have remuneration as high or higher for the noncollege or two-year college graduate as for the baccalaureate graduate, undoubtedly is based upon factual information. The implication that educational decisions should be made chiefly on that basis adds to the public confusion in interpreting the purposes of higher education.

Lack of timely and accurate information about the labor market has been a serious detriment in both personal and institutional decisions. The important need for the federal government to fill this informational gap has been emphasized by the National Board on Graduate Education. Its report, *Doctorate Manpower Forecasts and Policy* (November, 1973) documented shortcomings of the existing information base and inadequacies of current forecasting techniques. The analysis applies to other career lines as well. "Only the federal government has the capability and authority to collect consistent and comprehensive data on trends pertinent to the labor market for highly educated manpower, and we urge it to exercise this responsibility" (National Board on Graduate Education, 1974, p. 17).

In considering clues to the current public apathy, hostility, or skepticism toward the support of higher education, one is largely dependent on subjective evaluation. Much has been written but little proved about cause and effect; in time, more scholarly analysis will be available. Nevertheless, guidelines for tomorrow must be established with what we now observe and believe. There can be little doubt that the priority of the sixties, built upon wide public concern, confidence, and faith in the system, has been lost. Budgets tell the story, as do critics, commentators, polls, politicians, and the record of inadequate financial support.

Perhaps too much has been expected of faculties and graduates, or at least too much too soon. Perplexing problems remain, in spite of new knowledge and enlarged educational opportunity. Issues of war and peace, economic stability, and changing values create new anxieties. In identifying its programs with current urgencies, perhaps higher education has unwittingly encouraged false expectations. The linkages are real enough—to space science, race relations, urban affairs, ecology, energy, world food supply, better schools, the administration of justice, and others. But the time frame and the nature of the interactions have not always been made clear, nor has the fundamental mission of higher education—teaching, learning, inquiring, and applying knowledge—been meaningfully translated in human terms.

Whatever the causes, the priority granted to higher education in public policy concerns between 1960 and 1968 was lost. It is realistic, if not reassuring, to remember that the age of confidence was unusual and not very long. Those eight years cannot be regarded as the natural environment; they were simply the highest historic peak in the range of the hills and valleys of public esteem. There will be other peaks and valleys in the future. How high or low the priority depends in part on the reaction of the academic world itself to the new realities.

"Higher education in the United States has a remarkable

record of constructive adaptation to changing circumstances. . . . Now new challenges are being faced. . . . And higher education must now summon its many strengths to demonstrate once again, as it has so often in the past, that it is capable of self-renewal" (Kerr, 1975, pp. 6–7). If the system of higher education remains open and responsive to examination and to change, it will emerge from increased scrutiny and pressure with greater stability and more effective education and public service.

# 10

## Reflections for the Future

In looking at the stress, strain, and crisis in higher education from 1930–1970 as the backdrop for an unpredictable and uncertain future, three elements stand out: the oscillations in growth and their consequences; the constancy of change; the significance of public evaluation and the nature of public interaction.

### Analyzing Growth

When one charts the twentieth century enrolment peaks by decades, the graph line reflects continuous growth. This view obscures the tremendous and almost shocking oscillations that occurred after World Wars I and II, after the Depression, and in the fifties. For the institutions, the adjustments that had to be made in times of decline were as severe as in meeting the demands of the increase periods. Beyond the financial difficulties that always followed declines, the "down" periods inhibited creativity, planning, and constructive change. All of these changes were unanticipated and in each one the momentum of the previous period was slowed. This braking of momentum created deficits in resource acquisition and in educational development which were never completely overcome whether one looks at educational funding requirements, plant needs, unfulfilled desirable educational change, or relationships with the supporting society. The oscillations are important in understanding what happened; growth figures alone are misleading.

"Recovery lag" characterized higher education in the decades 1930–1970. After a dip in enrolment growth, the recovery did not go much beyond the earlier high point in the ratio of resources to commitments and obligations. A "catch-up" factor was always involved. What were perceived as necessary policy objectives always exceeded resources, particularly when such nonquantitative elements as quality, morale, creativity, and personal efficiency were considered. The new demands that arose were met in part by assimilation and adaptation, a fact obscured by increasing expenditures.

Although the period 1930–1970 appears to have been a time of steady growth, with proportionate accompanying successes in educational development and physical expansion, those who worked through those years remember them differently. Depression and War dominated the first two decades and basic survival was at stake for many institutions. The veteran enrolment spurts and the Tidal Wave were so overwhelming in demand for resources that a continuous struggle against inadequacy was normal. Conditions were not "affluent" or "golden" or "easy" in terms of quality maintenance and the effort toward improvement and greater effectiveness; the stresses and strains created apprehension and uncertainty as to the future. Faith on the part of the profession and many other supporters of higher education remained strong, but complacence was never in order. The movement toward mass higher education, then toward universal access, set the pace and the objectives were clear. The ways and means of the necessary additional resource acquisition were not clear, however. A closed college door was not an acceptable alternative if public confidence and corollary support were to be retained.

The tendency to associate growth in higher education with good times (public support and educational progress) and lack of growth with bad times (constraint and stagnation) is a superficial view. Such perspective overlooks the simple truth that growth can be harmful if underfunded and that it can distort purposes if not perceptively controled. Growth can also lead to inefficiency and the negative outcomes of loose management if growth pressures are unanticipated or responses unplanned. The adequacy of resources to perform an assigned mission is centrally influential on quality rather than growth.

To understand the 1930–1970 period, it is important to recognize that the development of higher education was horizontal as well as vertical. Over-all enrolment increase was dramatic, to be sure, but cost increase of services and functions not directly related to instruction was equally if not more dramatic. The funds expended on student aid, project research, and new public services took on new dimensions, but they had little effect on support required for "basic functions."[1]

As stated earlier, the term "affluence" is a misnomer as a description of the period. It is an error to apply the concept even in the sixties. The cost per student calculated upon costs for basic operations did not increase significantly beyond the normal rate of inflation. The notion that money for higher education was easy to get or that funds were available for the asking is an illusion; such an idea rests upon invalid comparisons and short memories. In a recent essay, lack of understanding is revealed by the use of the following terms as applicable to the sixties: "benign, extravagant, prosperous, lavish, golden years, blank checks." The author obviously had not faced an appropriation committee or built an institutional budget.

As the horizontal development progressed, it became apparent that a larger share of the national wealth would be required to underwrite the advance of higher education toward the goal of universal access. Halstead (1974, p. 528) has presented an analysis of this requirement in his description of a "capacity-burden ratio": "The fact that a larger percentage of young people than ever before are attending college is, of course, a consequence of efforts to achieve greater equality of access to higher education. However, when enrolment is viewed as a measure of financial burden, rapid growth becomes more a challenge than an achievement. The challenge can be observed in the fact that enrolment growth in higher education exceeds that of one of the common measures of ability to

[1] See Halstead (1974, p. 524) for a definition of basic functions.

pay—the nation's gross national product." The Gross National Product per full-time equivalent student declined in actual dollars from $170,725 in 1958 to $148,017 in 1971. When described in terms of constant (1967) dollars, the drop was even more dramatic: the amount of GNP per full-time equivalent student fell from $237,778 in 1958 to $111,880 in 1971. In Halstead's words, "The combined growth in the college-age group (4 percent annually), the college attendance ratio (3½ percent annually), and inflation (5½ percent annually) exceeded growth in the GNP (7½ percent annually)" (Halstead, 1974, pp. 535–536). These figures suggest that given the rapid increases in enrolments plus rising inflation from 1958 to 1971, an increasing proportion of the GNP was required *simply to maintain* on a much-expanded base the service level and program quality available in 1958.

Halstead also examines the amounts spent on general and administrative expenses during the same period. When viewed as a percentage of GNP, funds thus expended rose from approximately two-thirds of 1 percent in 1958 to 1.5 percent in 1971. When inflationary factors are taken into consideration, however, and a constant dollar figure is employed, the increase in per-student educational expenditures is quite small—from $1,542 per full-time equivalent student in 1958 to $1,621 per full-time equivalent student in 1971, or less than $100. O'Neil's earlier examination of productivity in higher education supports Halstead's findings. According to O'Neil (1971, p. 97) total instructional costs per credit hour in 1966–67, when measured in constant dollars for all institutions, remained virtually identical to the 1957–58 figure.

In generally assuming that higher education has not increased productivity over the years of expenditure acceleration, analysts have failed to take into account that in handling the tremendously enlarged load in enrolments and directly associated services, the unit cost in constant dollars, whether measured by credit hours or by capacity-burden ratio, has not increased significantly. Much remains to be done in clarifying the nature of expenditures, the relationship of restricted to unrestricted income, and the productivity involved in increasing scope of service while maintaining fairly constant unit costs. "But the truth of the matter is that most incremental spending in this period went to cover the cost of added functions—the establishment of graduate institutions on pre-existing collegiate bases; the re-equipping of the physical sciences and the adoption of new and elaborate research programs; the assumption of new responsibilities to the community and to the principle of equal access to education. On the whole, the academy is now paying not for having been overliberal, but for having been overtaxed" (Metzger, 1975, p. 27–28).

### Constancy of Change

The Educational Policies Commission wrote in 1951, "Fluctuating demands for higher education, in the last twenty years, have dealt a series of blows that would have sent less hardy and resilient institutions reeling to the mat" (Educational Policies Commission and others, 1951, p. 30). The fluctuations since 1951 justify extending the comment to the entire 40-year period.

The title of Brubacher and Rudy's *Higher Education in Transition,* spanning the 1636–1968 period, implies that higher education in the United States has been "in transition" from the beginning and that the conditions of the moment foretell further change. Although there has been a tendency to think of growth as the chief characteristic of higher education in the United States, the central and more compelling feature has really been continuous adaptation.

"Point-counterpoint," in providing a fairly consistent rationale for what happened in the past, suggests where the analysis of the 1970s and 1980s should be focused. Enrolment decrement and no-growth as contrasted with the traditional growth line invites change as surely as the conditions of other eras. History suggests that the planners for higher education in the decades ahead may count upon a continuation of the traditional capability for adaptation.

In dealing with resilience to stress and the capability for change, I do not imply that the change engendered is necessarily sound or good for the system, for society, or for the individual.

For example, that education has responded to the manpower demands of a technological age is quite clear; but whether the education of the individual has been improved by the subsuming of general education or whether personal values for adjusted living have been strengthened is another question. This demand and response interaction may be seen as reflective of the periods of calm as well as turmoil, those of war and depression, and those of growth and steady state.

That education responds to its environment is no new idea. Kolbe (1919, p. 5) in *Colleges in Wartime and After* made the point, "Certainly education from the earliest times has followed the leadership of economic necessity with almost slavish devotion." He then wove the theme into a description of higher education before World War I. The old idea requires reassertion, however, in the presence of modern critics who talk about "unresponsive" institutions and who shout alarms about the mismatch and disjointedness that invite catastrophe for the higher education system. Today's adaptation includes social as well as economic necessity.

Ashby has described the process: "The hope lies in step-by-step adaptation through the homeostatic mechanisms which respond to change as soon as change starts to bite" (Ashby, 1974, p. 145). In reflecting about change, its nature, and how it occurs, we may infer from Ashby that educational change follows external change and seldom operates in the reverse except in indirect and immeasurable ways. Sometimes the change is swept onto the scene by a major disturbance, as it has been in every time of war and in the Depression. Sputnik and the Tidal Wave provide other examples. Without such major disturbance in social equilibrium, change of lesser significance is precipitated in times of dialectic conflict or periods of diminished confidence.

It is important, if difficult, to remember that significant change usually can be effected and evaluated only over fairly long stretches of time. A specific change does not occur as soon as some would wish it, although change may come too rapidly for those who oppose it. How long is an appropriate period upon which to judge responsiveness—10, 20, 30 years? The

extreme critic usually demands instant change and is quick
to identify a scapegoat for his frustration when it does not
happen. Some significant changes have come on a relatively
short-term basis, but what is the normal expectation? We
really do not know much about the process of change—how
it starts, where the center of initiative is, how it is perceived
and hastened or retarded, and whether political power is the
cause or result. How does one determine when the "time has
come" for an idea?

A proposal for change may be around for a long time
before acceptance; most changes have had ideological roots
slow in growing. For example, after 20 years of considering
the use of technology in instruction, the idea still has not had
a major impact on the practices of colleges and universities.
Will another 10 years make a difference? As another example,
the Depression recovery established the presumption that colleges and universities had a role in adult education, to fill
in behind the federal emergency programs. In 1974, the college
role in adult education is still undefined.

Differentials in time intervals required for change are
to be expected. The preservation of traditional goals and functions is not necessarily an undesirable conservatism. Such
traditions come out of experience and are the result of testing
by trial and error. If there were not a struggle to conserve
goals and functions—if they were subject only to the standards
of "here and now" and "at once"—new values would not have
adequate appraisal and the building of consensus would be
the more difficult. Conflict and chaos would result.

Change must always be considered in terms of purposes
and goals. The debate should be on how best to advance purpose rather than change; much confusion arises because we
tend to debate change instead of purpose. To add to the difficulty, institutional goals change as they reflect conditions of
social change and changing public conceptions of progress.
But who speaks for "the people"? And how do "they" arrive
at consensus, that hinge of permanent change in a democratic
society? Similarly institutional adaptation must be supported
by internal consensus as well as consensus among external

constituencies that have interests at stake. Moreover, the diversity among institutions slows consensus building. "How to compose so many conflicting interests, and how to do so on a national scale which neglects no one of them, is to attempt a kind of rational planning that is still beyond the capacity of any administrative procedures that now exist" (Graubard, 1975, p. vii).

But the effort to find common ground among the institutions of higher education as the basis for public interpretation of purpose, achievement, and potential must go on in the drive for a higher public priority.

### Higher Education and the Public

While higher education in the United States may be viewed as an instrument of society and therefore affected in many ways by the external environment—in character, purpose, strength and structure—a complementary thesis must also be considered.

An influential force for constructive action in its entire history has been the widespread belief that higher education or advanced learning, including research, is "the engine of social progress." Sometimes the belief has been a matter of faith and conviction; sometimes, it has been based upon evidence of cause and effect. In either case, acceptance of the thesis has been the motivation for public policy in encouraging both institutions of higher education and the individual's pursuit of learning.

Whether the continuing expansion of the system may be traced to faith and conviction or to proof of social results is not the subject of this essay; yet there can be little doubt that higher education has survived periods of stress and crisis and gone on to new levels of achievement because the public has been aware of the interaction between higher education and social progress. In national emergencies of depression and war, the people have turned to organized higher education, its faculty and its graduates, for assistance. Even egalitarians, critical of the uneven distribution of benefits to individuals arising from advanced education, have accepted the essential intellectual elitism inherent in the search for talented students when it is accompanied by equality of opportunity and social justice for the individual.

It should be noted, too, that in the struggle to survive stress and crisis, great influence has been exerted by those who ardently, often eloquently, and persistently worked to interpret the social benefits of higher education. The search for public understanding should not be brushed aside on the assumption that the public benefits of "good works" are self-evident and compelling for support. Each informed observer of higher education development would have his own roll call of those whose voices were heard above contentious debate. But surely any list for the decades 1930–1970 would include Alfred North Whitehead, Samuel Capen, James Conant, Walter Lippman, John Gardner, James Reston, and Lyndon Johnson.

Increasingly, proof of accountability is expected and the academic commmunity will serve well in stimulating research on that subject and its interpretation. In self-interest, however, other segments of society—the professions, industry, consumers, labor, the devotees for improving the quality of life and achieving social justice—should also be evaluating the essentiality of advanced learning to the public welfare. An improving society is as much dependent upon higher education as the latter is upon social support. A main task of educational, civic, and political leadership in the period ahead should be to advance public recognition of this mutuality and interdependence. "Dependent on demography, dependent on the judgment of public authority, dependent upon the comparative performance of its competitors, dependent on the mercies of the mass media, open to the surrounding community, vulnerable to attacks against its own inadequacies, higher education today, as contrasted with a decade ago, is becoming more conscious that it is a subsystem within the total society and that it does not lead a life entirely of its own design" (Kerr, 1975, p. 3).

As a system, higher education has been less than ideally effective in communicating with the public. At every instance of crisis or stress, the general academic community has recognized the connection between public confidence and support, and considered briefly the ways and means of achieving public appreciation of goals, achievements, needs, and potential. Between those peaks of acute anxiety, however, the academic profession by and large has been indifferent, not even fully supportive of administrative efforts to build interpretative programs.

It is obvious for example, that students are graduated without having learned much about higher education as a system or as a social force in American life. Some disciplines touch upon the subject, but the membership of the student body as a whole is not seriously reached. As a result, alumni are usually not much better informed about the general higher education scene than their friends and associates who are not college graduates.

Even the professional preparation of faculty members does not include a familiarity with the history, nature, structure, economics, philosophy, and current condition of higher education. Obviously, on-the-job learning leaves much to be desired, and it scarcely provides faculty with motivation to introduce the subject to students as a lifetime interest. Reports of study commissions and recommendations of external agencies and groups, for example, seldom find a faculty audience except as the issues touch their own disciplines.

Apart from special communications from institutions, general information about higher education reaches the public through the mass media, reported in the main by nonspecialists. Coverage is limited to news or features that spotlight specific incidents or subjects. Business, government, sports, religion have their special writers with informed backgrounds. Higher education is treated sporadically and enjoys no such comprehensive and studied treatment.

A new factor enters into the interpretation dilemma as the current demand for accountability demonstrates the need for information that will be intelligible to nonprofessional audiences. One response should be greater attention by scholars to higher education as an area of study. A keen observer said recently: "Higher education needs desperately to be developed as a subject of sustained and deliberate scholarship. While no academic discipline can be established by fiat, many, in recent years, have been vastly expanded and modified through the insistence of public and private agencies that the subjects they treat are both too serious and too complex to depend on *ad hoc* and occasional inquiry" (Graubard, 1974, p. ix). The growing number of centers for the study of higher education and the increasing number of discipline approaches to such study are encouraging. But the activity must have the concern of the academic community as a whole if the findings are to have a place in communication channels for students, faculty, alumni, other special audiences, and the general public.

National professional institutional and discipline organizations should give this subject high priority in the consideration of graduate and undergraduate curriculum development at colleges and universities. The academic and administrative machinery at the institutional level will have to be much more involved than in the past in activity designed to gain adequate public understanding of the social importance of higher education. The range of possibilities is unlimited—from television and radio broadcasts to open houses for parents, neighbors, and special audiences; from continuing advisory committees to frequent special events.

How to improve communication is a large and complex subject. Past indifference and inertia cannot be overcome quickly. Responsibility centers in institutional action, although state, regional, and national agents have important roles in the process. Some advocate linking more closely academic contributions to specific national concerns, such as food, population, and energy (Boyer, 1974, p. 6). Others would stress the values and social benefits of intellectual freedom. "The ultimate criterion of the place of higher learning in America will be the extent to which it is esteemed not as a necessary instrument of external ends, but as an end in itself" (Hofstadter, 1952, p. 134). Obviously, the possible scope of approaches is broad, and probably both extremes and all in between are needed. The key requirement is that the effort be continuous with high priority for action at all levels and in all institutions.

In the end, of course, the process is meaningless without

substance. Program effectiveness and management efficiency must be at the heart of the effort.

### Variables in an Uncertain Future

The future of higher education is tied to public confidence in its mission and social contributions, and to its effectiveness in operation and management to achieve those ends. The sixties were not an age of affluence: Such strengthening as came to institutions arose from their being in an age of confidence. The present depression in higher education is traceable in part to economic conditions, but the degree of cutback is traceable to a loss of confidence. Similar experiences are reflected in every decade past.

Confidence is elusive and it is dependent on a host of variables. The role of the interpreters—leaders, scholars, trustees, citizen advocates—is vital. Such spokesmen can make a difference with opinion-makers, but whether these spokesmen are equal to the task at any given time of stress is a variable. Adequacy of communication is a factor, but the response of the academy in dealing with it is a variable. Attitudes of students, families, and special interests within the society affect general confidence, but their shifts are variables. "To what extent will women, blacks, certain ethnic minorities, and the poor look to higher education as the sure path out of poverty toward an improved socioeconomic status? To what extent will young men and women of the more affluent families look to higher education as an intellectual satisfaction rather than as a preparation for employment? To what extent will manpower planning come to dominate higher education?"[2] These are now pending questions, but their answers will be variables in the constant task of building confidence.

Then there will be those unforeseen climactic events that will affect the course of the nation, and with it the course of higher education. What will be the parallels to past wars and depressions; to the creation of radio and television; to atomic energy; to the moon shots and space exploration; to street riots;

[2] Letter to the author, John D. Millett, June 10, 1974.

to student disruption; to the shifts and turns of political leadership? These, too, will be variables in an unpredictable future.

But the constants are there, too. New knowledge and advanced learning are essential to a civilized society, regardless of the variables. As long as the technological society exists, the centrality of higher education will remain. Further, as attention is turned increasingly to the creation and expansion of human services within society, higher education will be called upon to train those who staff the service components. Optimism derived from these constants is more than the residue of an old-fashioned faith. It is a realistic acknowledgment of where we are, and it can be grounds for confidence despite the variables.

# References

"AAUP General Secretary Report of 1939." *AAUP Bulletin*, 1939, *25*, 13–14.

Adams, A. S. "Faith in the People." In R. F. Howes (Ed.), *Causes of Public Unrest Pertaining to Education*. Washington, D.C.: American Council on Education, 1953.

American Assembly. *The Federal Government and Higher Education*. Englewood Cliffs, N.J.: Prentice-Hall, 1960.

American Association of University Professors. *Depression, Recovery and Higher Education*. New York: McGraw-Hill, 1937.

American Council on Education. *Supplementary Statements on Education and National Security*. Washington, D.C., 1952.

American Council on Education. *A Call for Action to Meet the Impending Increase in College and University Enrollment*. Washington, D.C., 1954.

American Council on Education. *Action Under Way to Meet the Rising Tide of Enrollment in American Colleges and Universities*. Washington, D.C., 1955.

American Council on Education. *A Fact Book on Higher Education*. Issue 1, Enrollment Data. Washington, D.C., 1974.

Armsby, H. H. *Engineering, Science, and Management War Training Program: Final Report*, U.S. Office of Education Bulletin 9. Washington, D.C.: U.S. Government Printing Office, 1946.

Ashby, E. *Any Person, Any Study*. New York: McGraw-Hill, 1971.

Ashby, E. *Adapting Universities to a Technological Society*. San Francisco: Jossey-Bass, 1974.

Association of American Universities. "The Rights and Responsibilities of Universities and Their Faculties." Washington, D.C., 1953, 1962.

Auburn, N. "Life, Liberty, and Higher Learning." *American Alumni Council News*, Sept. 1958, *26*, p. 17.

Badger, H. G. *The Economic Outlook in Higher Education for 1934–35*, U.S. Office of Education Pamphlet 58. Washington, D.C.: U.S. Government Printing Office, 1934.

Balderston, F. E. *Managing Today's University*. San Francisco: Jossey-Bass, 1974.

Baumol, W. and Heim, P. "The Economic Status of the Academic Profession: Taking Stock 1964–65." *AAUP Bulletin,* Summer 1965, *51,* 248–301.

Ben-David, J. *American Higher Education: Directions Old and New.* New York: McGraw-Hill, 1972.

Bolman, F. deW., Jr. "Universal Military Service and Training—An Educational Opportunity?" *School and Society,* Apr. 14, 1951, *73,* 229–232.

Bowyer, C. H. *The Directory of Education Associations.* Emporia, Kan.: Kansas State Teachers College Press, 1962.

Boyer, E. L., as cited in P. W. Semas, "Universities and Government." *Chronicle of Higher Education,* Nov. 25, 1974, *9,* p. 6.

Brandon, A. L. *Postwar Education in American Colleges and Universities, A Survey Report.* Bloomington, Ind.: American College Publicity Association, 1944.

Brown, F. J. (Ed.) *Emergency Problems in Higher Education,* Series 1, Reports of Committees and Conferences, *10* (24). Washington, D.C.: American Council on Education, 1946.

Brown, F. J. "Post-War Development." In P. F. Valentine (Ed.), *The American College.* New York: Philosophical Library, Inc., 1949.

Brown, F. J. "A Long-Range View of Higher Education." *The Annals,* Sept. 1955, *301,* 1–6.

Brown, F. J. (Ed.) *Issues in Education,* Series 1, Reports of Committees and Conferences, *14* (43). Washington, D.C.: American Council on Education, 1950.

Brown, F. J. (Ed.) *Higher Education in the National Service,* Series 1, Reports of Committees and Conferences, *14* (44). Washington, D.C.: American Council on Education, 1950.

Brown, F. J. (Ed.) *National Defense and Higher Education,* Series 1, Reports of Committees and Conferences, *15* (47). Washington, D.C.: American Council on Education, 1951.

Brown, F. J. and Sellin, T. (Eds.) "Higher Education Under Stress." *The Annals,* Sept. 1955, *301,* Special Issue.

Brubacher, J. S. and Rudy, W. *Higher Education in Transition: A History of American Colleges and Universities, 1636–1968.* New York: Harper & Row, 1968.

Burns, J. MacG. (Ed.) *To Heal and to Build: The Programs of President Lyndon B. Johnson.* New York: McGraw-Hill, 1968.

Carnegie Commission on Higher Education. *Quality and Equality: New Levels of Federal Responsibility for Higher Education.* New York: McGraw-Hill, Dec. 1968.

Carnegie Commission on Higher Education. *The More Effective Uses of Resources.* New York: McGraw-Hill, 1972.

Carnegie Commission on Higher Education. *Higher Education: Who Pays? Who Benefits? Who Should Pay?* New York: McGraw-Hill, 1973a.

Carnegie Commission on Higher Education. *Priorities for Action: Final Report of the Carnegie Commission on Higher Education.* New York: McGraw-Hill, 1973b.

Cheit, E. F. *The New Depression in Higher Education.* New York: McGraw-Hill, 1971.

Cheit, E. F. *The New Depression in Higher Education—Two Years Later.* New York: McGraw-Hill, 1973.

Christiansen, J. D. "University and College Finances During the Depression." *School and Society,* June 9, 1934, *39,* 729–735.

Commission on Financing Higher Education. *Final Report: Nature and Needs of Higher Education.* New York: Columbia University Press, 1952.

Committee Z on the Economic Status of the Profession. "The Threat of Inflationary Erosion." *AAUP Bulletin,* June 1969, *55,* 192–253.

Committee Z on the Economic Status of the Profession. "Rising Costs and the Public Institutions." *AAUP Bulletin,* June 1970, *56,* 174–239.

Conant, J. B. *My Several Lives.* New York: Harper & Row, 1970.

Cook, F. J. *The Nightmare Decade,* The Life and Times of Senator Joe McCarthy. New York: Random House, 1971.

Council for Financial Aid to Education, Inc. *Voluntary Support of Education, 1971–1972.* New York, 1972.

Cremin, L. A. *American Education: The Colonial Experience, 1607–1783.* New York: McGraw-Hill, 1970.

Davidson, C. "Government Support of Private Colleges and Universities." *The Annals,* Sept. 1955, *301,* 112–122.

DeKiewiet, C. W. "How Different Types of Institutions are Planning for the Future." *Action Underway to Meet the Rising Tide of Enrolment in American Colleges and Universities.* Washington, D.C.: American Council on Education, 1955.

DeMello, D. *The McCarthy Era: 1950–54.* New York: Scholastic Book Services, 1968.

Dobbins, C. G. (Ed.) *The Strength to Meet our National Need.* Washington, D.C.: American Council on Education, 1956.

Dobbins, C. G. (Ed.) *American Council on Education: Leadership and Chronology, 1918–1968.* Washington, D.C.: American Council on Education, 1968.

Dresch, S. P. *An Economic Perspective on the Evolution of Graduate Education.* National Board on Graduate Education, Technical Report 1. Washington, D.C., Mar. 1974.

Drucker, P. F. "The Promise of Automation." *Harper's Magazine,* Apr. 1955, *210,* 41–47.

Educational Policies Commission. *Education and the People's Peace.* Washington, D.C.: National Education Association of the United States, 1943.

Educational Policies Commission. *American Education and International Tensions.* Washington, D.C.: National Education Association of the United States and the American Association of School Administrators, 1949.

Educational Policies Commission. *Higher Education in a Decade of Decision.* Washington, D.C.: National Education Association of the United States and the American Association of School Administrators, 1957.

Educational Policies Commission of the National Education Association, American Association of School Administrators, and the Executive Committee of the American Council on Education. *Education and National Security.* Washington, D.C., 1951.

Educational Testing Service. *Final Report on Educational Assistance to Veterans: A Comparative Study of Three G.I. Bills.* Washington, D.C.: U.S. Government Printing Office, 1973.

Farrell, A. P. "Report of the President's Commission: A Critical Appraisal." In G. Kennedy (Ed.), *Education for Democracy.* Boston: D. C. Heath, 1952.

*Ferment in Education, the Problems, Responsibilities, and Opportunities of Universities at This Time.* A Symposium at the Installation of George Dinsmore Stoddard as President of the University of Illinois. Urbana, Ill.: University of Illinois Press, 1948.

Frederikson, N. and Schrader, W. B. *Adjustment to College.* Princeton, N.J.: Educational Testing Service, 1951.

Freeman, R. B. and Breneman, D. W. *Forecasting the Ph.D. Labor Market: Pitfalls for Policy.* Washington, D.C.: National Board on Graduate Education, Apr. 1974.

Glenny, L. A. "The Illusions of Steady State." *Change Magazine.* Winter, 1974–75, *6,* 24–28.

Grace, A. *Educational Lessons from Wartime Training,* The General Report of the Commission on Implications of Armed Services Educational Programs. Washington, D.C.: American Council on Education, 1948.

Graubard, S. R. (Ed.) *American Higher Education: Toward An Uncertain Future,* Vol. I. Daedalus, Fall 1974, *103,* Entire Issue.

Graubard, S. R. (Ed.) *American Higher Education: Toward An Uncertain Future.* Vol. II. Daedalus, Winter 1975, *104,* Entire Issue.

Griffith, R. *The Politics of Fear,* Joseph R. McCarthy and the Senate. Lexington, Ky.: The University Press of Kentucky, 1970.

Halstead, D. *Statewide Planning in Higher Education.* Department of Health, Education and Welfare Publication (OE) 73-17001. Washington, D.C.: U.S. Government Printing Office, 1974.

Handlin, O. and Handlin, M. F. *The American College and American Culture.* New York: McGraw-Hill, 1970.

Harris, S. E. "Millions of B.A.'s, But No Jobs." In G. Kennedy (Ed.), *Education for Democracy.* Boston: D. C. Heath, 1952.

Harris, S. E. *A Statistical Portrait of Higher Education.* New York: McGraw-Hill, 1972.

Henderson, A. "The Market for College Graduates: A Review." In G. Kennedy (Ed.), *Education for Democracy.* Boston: D. C. Heath, 1952, 72–80.

Henderson, A. D. "Contrasting Principles in Higher Education." *School and Society,* Mar. 28, 1953, *77,* p. 195.

Henry, D. D. *What Priority for Education? The American People Must Soon Decide.* Urbana, Ill.: University of Illinois Press, 1961.

Henry, D. D. "Accountability: To Whom, For What, By What Means?" *Educational Record,* Fall 1972, *53,* 287–292.

Higher Education and the War, The Report of a National Conference of College and University Presidents, held in Baltimore, Md., January 3–4, 1942. Washington, D.C.: American Council on Education, 1942.

Hill, D. S., Kelly, F. J., and Savage, H. J. *Economy in Higher Education.* New York: The Carnegie Foundation for the Advancement of Teaching, 1933.

Hofstadter, R. "The Development of Higher Education in America." In R. Hofstadter and C. DeW. Hardy, *The Development and Scope of Higher Education in the United States.* New York: Columbia University Press, 1952.

Hollinshead, B. S. "Colleges of Freedom." In G. Kennedy (Ed.), *Education for Democracy.* Boston: D. C. Heath, 1952, 81–89.

Hollis, E. and Flynt, R. C. M. *Higher Education Looks Ahead,* U.S. Office of Education Bulletin 8. Washington, D.C.: U.S. Government Printing Office, 1945.

Howes, R. F. (Ed.) *Causes of Public Unrest Pertaining to Education,* Series 1, Reports of Committees and Conferences, *17* (56). Washington, D.C.: American Council on Education, 1953.

Hutchins, R. M. "Double Trouble: Are More Studies, More Facilities, More Money the Key for Better Education?" In G. Kennedy (Ed.), *Education for Democracy.* Boston: D. C. Heath, 1952, 81–89.

Kaysen, C. (Ed.) *Content and Context.* New York: McGraw-Hill, 1973.

Kennedy, G. (Ed.) *Education for Democracy,* The Debate Over the Report of the President's Commission on Higher Education. Boston: D. C. Heath, 1952.

Kerr, C. *The Uses of the University: With a "Postscript—1972."* Cambridge, Mass.: Harvard University Press, 1972.

Kerr, C. "What We Might Learn from the Climacteric." *Daedalus,* Winter 1975, *104,* 1–7.

Kolbe, P. R. *The Colleges in War Time and After.* New York: D. Appleton, 1919.

Lazarsfeld, P. F. and Thielens, W. Jr. *The Academic Mind.* Glenco, Ill.: Free Press, 1958.

Leslie, L., and Miller, H. Jr. *Higher Education and the Steady State.* Washington, D.C.: ERIC Clearinghouse on Higher Education, 1974.

Lindley, B. and Lindley, E. K. *A New Deal For Youth.* New York: Viking Press, 1938.

Lipset, S. M. *Rebellion in the University.* Boston, Mass.: Little, Brown, 1971.

Long, H. J. "What Are the Private Colleges Doing to Meet the Crisis Ahead?" *School and Society,* June 30, 1951, *73,* 410–411.

McConnell, T. R. "A Reply to the Critics." In G. Kennedy (Ed.), *Education for Democracy.* Boston: D. C. Heath, 1952.

McConnell, T. R. and Willey, M. M. (Eds.) *Higher Education and the War. The Annals,* Jan. 1944, *231,* 1–162.

Metzger, W. P. "The American Academic Profession in 'Hard Times.'" *Daedalus,* Winter 1975, *104,* 25–44.

Miller, J. and Brooks, D. V. N. *The Role of Higher Education in War and After.* New York: Harper & Row, 1944.

Millett, J. D. *Financing Higher Education in the United States,* Staff Report of the Commission on Financing Higher Education. New York: Columbia University Press, 1952.

Millett, J. D. *Politics and Higher Education.* University, Ala.: University of Alabama Press, 1974.

Millett, J. D. "Recent Developments in Financing Higher Education." *The Annals,* Sept. 1955, *301,* 205–210.

Morey, L. "Finance and Business Administration in Institutions of Higher Education." *Review of Educational Research,* Apr. 1935, *5,* 143–147.

Morrill, J. L. "Higher Education and the Federal Government." *The Annals,* Sept. 1955, *301,* 41–45.

Morison, S. E. *Harvard College in the Seventeenth Century.* Two Volumes. Cambridge, Mass.: Harvard University Press, 1936.

Moulton, H. G. "The University and Governmental Changes." *Scientific Monthly,* Jan. 1933, *36,* p. 40.

Moynihan, D. P. "The Politics of Higher Education." *Daedalus,* Winter 1975, *104,* 128–147.

Murphy, F. D. "The Real Meaning of the Satellite." *Educational Record,* Jan. 1958, *39,* 35–36.

National Board on Graduate Education. *Doctorate Manpower Forecasts and Policy.* Washington, D.C.: National Academy of Sciences, Nov. 1973.

National Board on Graduate Education. *Federal Policy Alternatives Toward Graduate Education.* Washington, D.C.: National Academy of Sciences, Jan. 1974.

National Center for Education Statistics. *Digest of Educational Statistics, 1973 Edition,* Department of Health, Education and Welfare Publication (OE) 74-11103. Washington, D.C.: U.S. Government Printing Office, 1974.

*The New York Times.* "WPA Training More than All Colleges." Dec. 13, 1936, p. 47.

Nisbet, R. *The Degradation of the Academic Dogma: The University in America 1945–1970.* New York: Basic Books, 1971.

Olson, K. W. *The G.I. Bill, the Veterans, and the Colleges.* Lexington, Ky.: University of Kentucky Press, 1974.

O'Neil, J. *Resource Use in Higher Education,* Trends in Output and Input, 1930–1967. Berkeley, Calif.: Carnegie Commission on Higher Education, 1971.

Orlans, H. *The Effects of Federal Programs on Higher Education.* Washington, D.C.: The Brookings Institution, 1962.

Perkins, J. A. "Government Support of Public Universities and Colleges." *The Annals,* Sept. 1955, *301,* 101–111.

Pifer, A. *The Nature and Origins of the Carnegie Commission on Higher Education.* New York: Carnegie Commission on Higher Education, 1972.

President's Advisory Committee on Education. *The Report of the Committee.* Washington, D.C.: U.S. Government Printing Office, 1939.

President's Commission on Higher Education. *Higher Education for American Democracy,* Vol. 1–6. New York: Harper & Row, 1947.

President's Commission on Veteran's Pensions. *Readjustment Benefits: Education and Training, and Employment and Unemployment,* Staff Report 9, Part B. Washington, D.C.: U.S. Government Printing Office, 1956.

President's Committee on Education Beyond the High School. *First Interim Report to the President.* Washington, D.C.: U.S. Government Printing Office, 1956.

President's Committee on Education Beyond the High School. *Second Report to the President.* Washington, D.C.: U.S. Government Printing Office, 1957.

Pusey, N. M. *The Age of the Scholar.* Cambridge, Mass.: The Belknap Press of Harvard University Press, 1963.

Pusey, N. M. "The Carnegie Study of the Federal Government and Higher Education." In C. G. Dobbins (Ed.), *Higher Education and the Federal Government.* Papers presented at the Forty-fifth Annual Meeting of the American Council on Education. Washington, D.C.: American Council on Education, 1962.

Quattlebaum, C. A. *Federal Educational Policies, Programs and Proposals: A Survey and Handbook.* Washington, D.C.: U.S. Government Printing Office, 1968.

Quattlebaum, C. A. "Federal Policies and Practices in Higher Education." In American Assembly, *The Federal Government and Higher Education.* Englewood Cliffs, N.J.: Prentice-Hall, 1960.

Rivlin, A. M. *The Role of the Federal Government in Financing Higher Education.* Washington, D.C.: The Brookings Institution, 1961.

Ross, D. R. B. *Preparing for Ulysses: Politics and Veterans During World War II.* New York: Columbia University Press, 1969.

Rudolph, F. *The American College and University: A History.* New York: Vintage Books, 1962.

Russell, J. D. (Ed.) "The Outlook for Higher Education." *Proceedings of the Institute for Administrative Officers of Higher Education,* Vol. 11. Chicago: The University of Chicago Press, 1939.

Russell, J. D. (Ed.) "Higher Education in the Postwar Period." *Proceedings of the Institute for Administrative Officers,* Vol. 16. Chicago: University of Chicago Press, 1946.

Russell, J. D. (Ed.) "Emergent Responsibilities in Higher Education." *Proceedings of the Institute for Administrative Officers,* Vol. 17. Chicago: University of Chicago Press, 1946.

Sachar, A. L. "Educational Administrators in Today's World." In R. F. Howes (Ed.), *Causes of Public Unrest Pertaining to Education.* Washington, D.C.: American Council on Education, 1953.

Solberg, W. U. *The University of Illinois, 1867–1894: An Intellectual and Cultural History.* Urbana, Ill.: University of Illinois Press, 1968.

Stoke, H. W. "The Flowering Curricula of American Higher Education." *The Annals,* Sept. 1955, *301,* 58–64.

Superintendent of Public Instruction of the State of Michigan. *Ninety-Second Biennial Report, 1931–1933.* Lansing, Mich.: Franklin Dekline, 1934.

Tewksbury, D. G. *The Founding of American Colleges and Universities Before the Civil War.* New York: Archon Books, 1965.

Thompson, R. B. "College Age Population Trends." *College and University,* Jan. 1954, *29,* 4, 215–224.

Thompson, R. B. "The Need for Expanded Facilities." In C. Dobbins (Ed.), *The Strength to Meet Our National Need.* Washington, D.C.: American Council on Education, 1956, 93–98.

Thwing, C. F. *The American Colleges and Universities in the Great War.* New York: Macmillan, 1920.

Trytten, M. H. "Meeting Manpower Needs." *The Annals,* Sept. 1955, *301,* 17–21.

U.S. Department of Health, Education and Welfare. *Grants-in Aid and Other Financial Assistance Programs.* Washington, D.C.: U.S. Government Printing Office, 1967, 60–63.

U.S. Department of Health, Education and Welfare. *Catalog of HEW Assistance.* Washington, D.C.: U.S. Government Printing Office, 1969.

U.S. Office of Education. *Biennial Survey of Education in the United States.* Washington, D.C.: U.S. Government Printing Office. Published biennially from 1916–1918 to 1956–1958.

U.S. Office of Education. *Opening Fall Enrollment in Higher Education, 1955.* Circular 460. Washington, D.C.: Government Printing Office, 1956.

Valentine, P. F. (Ed.) *The American College.* San Francisco: Philosophical Library, 1949.

Veysey, L. R. *The Emergence of the American University.* Chicago: The University of Chicago Press, 1965.

Veysey, L. R. "Stability and Experiment in the American Undergraduate Curriculum." In C. Kaysen (Ed.), *Content and Context.* New York: McGraw-Hill, 1973, 1–63.

Walters, R. "Statistics of Registration of Thirty American Universities for 1920." *School and Society,* Jan. 29, 1920, *13,* 121–128.

Walters, R. "Higher Education in the National Emergency." *AAUP Bulletin,* Spring 1951, *37,* 31–40.

War Manpower Commission. *Final Report of the National Youth Administration,* Fiscal Years 1936–1943. Washington, D.C.: U.S. Government Printing Office, 1944.

Weekly Compilation of Presidential Documents, Nov. 15, 1965, *1,* 67–496.

Wilson, Logan (Ed.) *Emerging Patterns in American Higher Education.* Washington, D.C.: American Council on Education, 1965.

Zook, G. F. "How the Colleges Went to War." *The Annals,* Jan. 1944, *231,* 1–7.

Zook, G. F. "Summary of the Effects of the War on Institutions of Higher Education." In J. D. Russell (Ed.), "Higher Education Under War Conditions," *Proceedings of the Institute for Administrative Officers,* Vol. 15. Chicago: University of Chicago Press, 1943, 145–159.

# Index